To the mothers in my life, past and present,
who taught me the most important lesson of all:
this journey is my own.

Intentional Motherhood: Transforming Challenges into Growth Opportunities

Published by Denotion Research Group

www.DenotionResearch.com

ISBN:

978-1-958634-25-7 (Hardcover)

978-1-958634-27-1 (Paperback)

978-1-958634-26-4 (eBook)

Printed in United States 1st Edition

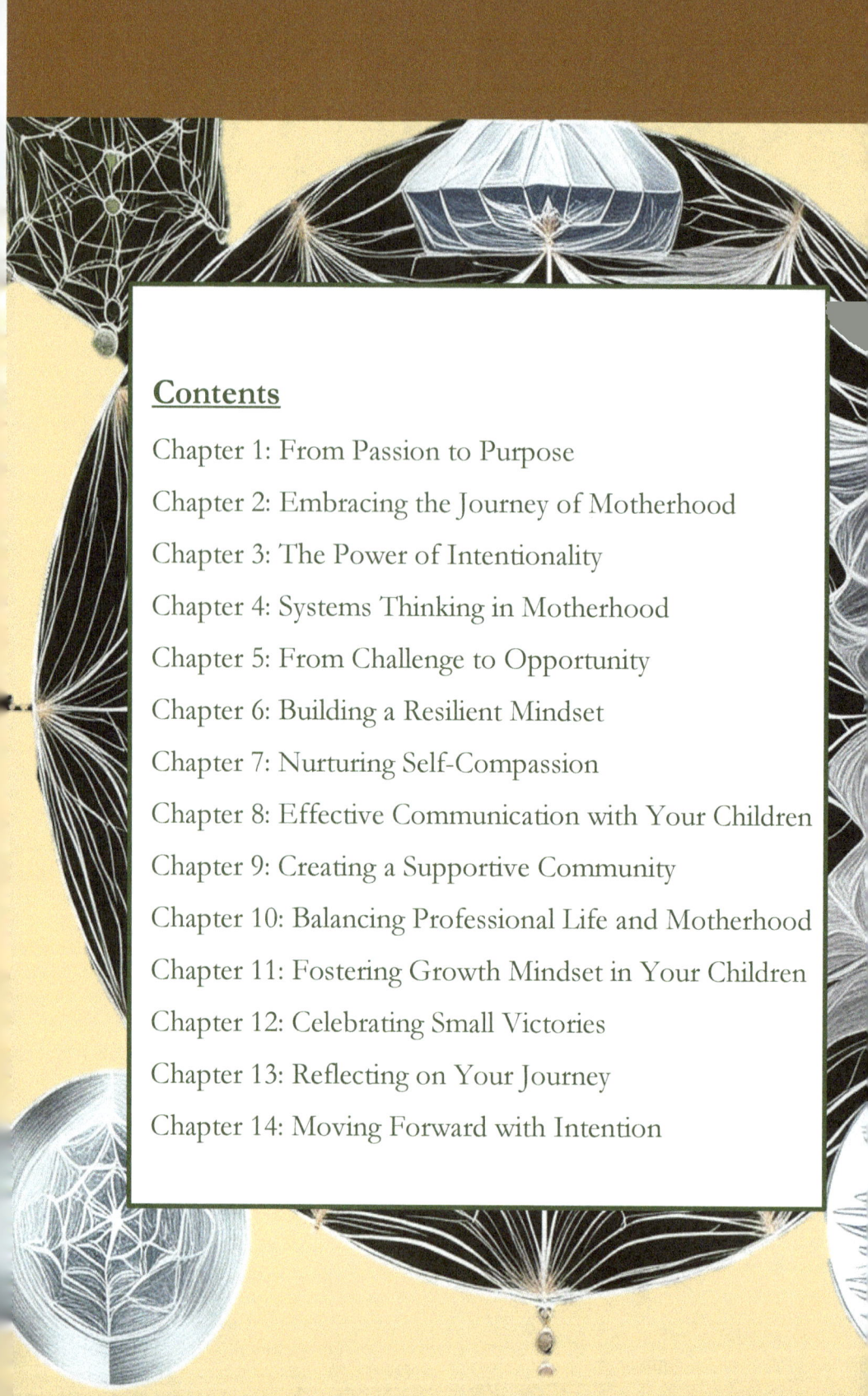

Contents

Chapter 1:
From Passion to Purpose

"Motherhood, in its purest form, is not about self-sacrifice, but about self-actualization. It's about discovering your own passions and nurturing them alongside your children, showing them that a fulfilling life is a complex system derived from love, purpose, and the unwavering pursuit of one's dreams."

— Dr. Federica Robinson-Bryant

Discovering My "Why"

Two decades ago, if you had asked me who I envisioned myself becoming, "mother" wouldn't have made the list. As I pursued a demanding academic path, filled with engineering degrees and a passion for travel and exploration, the world of diapers and family carpools felt like an altogether foreign land. Yet, life has a way of surprising us, doesn't it? Today, I proudly wear the title of mother to four incredible children—ages 5, 10, 12, and 16— each of whom has profoundly shaped my identity and priorities.

In reflecting on my journey, I realize that my initial reluctance to embrace motherhood was steeped in misconceptions. I often thought of motherhood as a role that required innate skills and desires, I believed I lacked. But as it turns out, the stereotypical qualities of nurturing and unconditional love activated within me on that warm spring day, as my first child entered the world. That unexpected pregnancy coincided with my undergraduate studies, marking the beginning of my professional journey while simultaneously introducing me to the beautiful chaos of motherhood. I graduated mere days after her birth, donning my cap and gown with a mix of pride and trepidation, stepping into a new chapter that would ultimately redefine success.

With each passing year, my life has been a delicate balancing act between professional aspirations and the demands of family life. I earned two master's degrees and a doctorate, carved out a career as an associate professor and administrator in a leading institution, contributed as a systems engineer for the federal government, and served as a research administrator for social and emotional learning programming across a local school district.

Yet, as the accolades and more technical outcomes piled up, the more I understood the dynamics of the systems around me. The naive sense of fulfillment in serving my scientific community and the priorities of others, left a trail of heartbreak and a void in my mind and spirit.

I came to realize that the core of who I am was being drawn in a different direction—back to my role as a mother and my devotion to the generations to come. I discovered that the greatest satisfaction came not from career titles or engineering marvels but from nurturing the lives of children.

In those quiet moments of connection, whether through the creation of memorable moments or shared laughter, I realized that the true measure of success lies in the love and values we pass on, shaping the future one child at a time. This journey of motherhood has not only deepened my understanding of the world but has also inspired me to rethink what it truly means to lead a fulfilling life.

My journey hasn't been without its hurdles. I've navigated the challenges of a pandemic, the complexities of divorce, and the emotional toll of loss—all while striving to be the mother my children deserve. I've faced burnout, self-doubt, and the relentless pressure to do it all for everyone, often at the expense of my own well-being. But through it all, I've learned that intentionality is key. This realization inspired the creation of this book, "Intentional Motherhood," which serves as both a personal reflection and a practical guide for other women navigating the intricate dance of ambition and nurturing.

I want to emphasize that I do not claim to be an expert in motherhood; rather, a woman navigating her own unique journey, just like you. We all face challenges, moments of doubt, and the occasional struggle, and it's important to remember that we are in this together. So, if you ever see me out in the world, grappling with the ups and downs of parenting, please extend to me the same grace and understanding that you should offer yourself. We are all learning, growing, and doing our best, and it is this shared experience that connects us as mothers. Let's commit to supporting one another in our journeys, recognizing that none of us has all the answers, but together, we can find strength and encouragement in our imperfections.

In these pages, I'll share the strategies that have helped me redefine motherhood as not simply a series of reactions to daily demands but as an intentional journey shaped by love and purpose. This book will explore:

- ❖ *Prioritizing with Purpose:* Discovering how to align your actions with your values, so you can say "no" to what drains you and "yes" to what fuels you.

- ❖ *Cultivating Mindfulness:* Learning to be present in the whirlwind of daily life, savoring the small moments that matter most.

- ❖ *Building Strong Foundations:* Nurturing healthy relationships within your family, emphasizing open communication and emotional support.

- ❖ *Practicing Self-Care:* Understanding that caring for yourself is not selfish; it's essential for being the best mother you can be.

This isn't just a theoretical framework; it's a culmination of my own experiences— the triumphs, the struggles, and the lessons learned along the way.

We will begin by crafting your own "Motherhood Manifesto," a living document that encapsulates your core values, priorities, and aspirations as a mother. This manifesto serves as a guiding light in your parenting journey, allowing you to articulate your beliefs about motherhood and the principles that will shape your approach to raising your children. As you reflect on your unique experiences, consider the qualities you wish to instill in your children, the lessons you want to impart, and the legacy you hope to create.

Take some time to think about what motherhood means to you—what moments have been most significant, what challenges have shaped your perspective, and what joys you cherish. You might explore themes such as compassion, resilience, creativity, or independence, and how these values can manifest in your daily interactions. Once you have a clear vision, you will be guided through the process of writing your manifesto. Consider adding personal anecdotes, quotes, or artistic elements to deepen the sentiment of this exercise.

MOTHERHOOD *Manifesto*

What are your key values as a mother?

List your near-term priorities
along your parenting journey:

1. _____
2. _____
3. _____

List your long-term aspirations
along your motherhood journey:

1. _____
2. _____
3. _____

Develop a goal statement to use as your grounding and guide as a mother.

Add something personal over this
space, e.g. a quote, family picture,
or anything that may have
sentimental value to you.

Latest Update

This manifesto will not only serve as a reminder of your intentions but can also be revisited and revised as your children grow and your understanding of motherhood evolves. By the end of this activity, you will leave with a tangible reflection of your motherhood journey, a source of inspiration that you can refer to whenever you need to reconnect with your purpose and values as a parent.

The structure of this book is designed to foster deep and meaningful engagement with the concepts of intentional motherhood. Each chapter is crafted to encourage not only learning but also reflection and action, ensuring that you don't just skim the surface but dig deep into your own experiences and values. Therefore, I caution and emphasize that this book is not intended to be a quick read; rather, it invites you to take your time, reflect on your insights, and implement new strategies in your life.

Throughout the text, you will find numerous worksheets that prompt personal exploration, allowing you to create accountability and actionable plans tailored to your unique journey. All of the activities are thoughtfully designed with 14 Areas of Systems Thinking (ASTS) in mind, ensuring that each exercise not only fosters engagement but also deepens understanding of the inherent interconnectedness. By integrating these ASTS principles, the activities encourage you to explore multiple perspectives, recognize dynamic behaviors, and acknowledge the complexities of relationships within family systems.

Additionally, I have included at least one activity at the end of each chapter that you can complete with your family, fostering connection and shared growth as you navigate the beautiful complexities of motherhood together. You'll discover that this journey is not just about individual transformation but also about enriching your family bonds, building a sense of community, and creating lasting memories.

I invite you to join me on this journey—embracing the challenges, celebrating the victories, and cultivating a life of intentionality that enriches both your motherhood and your soul. Through much reflection and process, we will redefine what it means to be an intentional mother, creating a legacy of love and purpose for ourselves and our children.

Family Engagement Opportunity

Family Photo

Gather your family together for a special photo session that captures the essence of your unique bond and shared journey. Choose a meaningful location—perhaps your favorite park, a cozy spot in your home, or a place that holds special memories for your family. Before taking the picture, take a moment to discuss what makes your family unique and what you appreciate about one another. Pose in a way that reflects your personalities, whether it's a silly group shot, a candid moment, or a more formal portrait. Once the photo is taken, display it prominently in your home as a reminder of your collective journey and the connections you share.

Chapter 2:
Embracing the Journey of Motherhood

"The most beautiful experience we can experience is the
mysterious. It is the source of all true art and science. He to whom
this emotion is a stranger, who can no longer pause to wonder and
stand rapt in awe, is as good as dead: his eyes are closed."

— Albert Einstein

The Beauty of Imperfection

The journey of parenthood is often painted with the brushstrokes of perfectionism. Society tends to set lofty expectations for how we should raise our children, the milestones they should reach, and the kind of parents we should be. Yet, within the chaotic and sometimes messy reality of family life lies an undeniable truth: perfection is an illusion. Embracing the beauty of imperfection allows us to foster a nurturing environment where both parents and children can grow, learn, and thrive. It is in our flaws and missteps that the most profound lessons emerge, teaching us resilience, empathy, and the power of connection.

In learning to accept imperfection, we open ourselves to the richness of experience. Each mistake or unexpected turn in our parenting journey is an opportunity for growth. When we let go of the need to be flawless, we create space for authenticity. This authenticity not only strengthens our relationship with our children but also models for them the importance of embracing their own imperfections. When children see their parents navigating challenges with grace and humor, they learn that it is okay to stumble and that mistakes are simply stepping stones on the path to self-discovery.

The beauty of imperfection also lies in the unique perspectives it offers. Every family is a complex web with different threads of personality, experiences, and values. When we allow ourselves to be imperfect, we invite diversity into our lives. This diversity enriches our family dynamics and opens up discussions about acceptance, understanding, and growth. By celebrating our differences and recognizing that no two journeys are the same, we teach our children the value of both individuality and teams, and the strength found in vulnerability.

Moreover, embracing imperfection cultivates compassion—not just towards ourselves but also towards others. In a world that often encourages comparison, recognizing that everyone struggles with their own set of challenges helps us build a supportive community. As parents and professionals, we can create spaces where we uplift one another, sharing our stories of hardship and triumph. This sense of community nurtures resilience, reminding us that we are not alone in our struggles and that every challenge faced is a chance to grow together.

Ultimately, the beauty of imperfection is a powerful reminder that life is not about achieving a perfect outcome but about the journey we take along the way. Each moment of joy, sorrow, success, and failure shapes us and our children into the individuals we are meant to be. By embracing imperfection, we not only transform our own lives but also empower the next generation to approach their challenges with courage and creativity. In doing so, we foster a legacy of resilience, acceptance, and love, ensuring that our families thrive in their beautifully imperfect way.

In our next activity, I invite you to take a reflective journey by focusing on a single mistake you feel you made as a mother. This exercise is not about dwelling on guilt or regret, but rather about embracing the opportunity for growth and understanding that comes from acknowledging our missteps. Motherhood is a complex and often challenging experience, and we all stumble along the way. By identifying one particular mistake, you can gain valuable insights into how it has shaped both you and your children.

As you think about this mistake, consider what you learned from the experience. Was it a lesson about patience, communication, or perhaps the importance of vulnerability? Reflecting on the lessons can help you recognize your own growth as a parent, illustrating how challenges can foster resilience and adaptability. Additionally, think about what your children may have learned from this situation. Children are perceptive and often pick up on the nuances of our interactions, so understanding their perspective can provide clarity on how these moments influence their development and worldview.

Finally, we will explore the impact of this mistake on your relationship with your children. Did it create a moment of connection or distance? How did it affect your communication and trust? By examining these dynamics, you can better understand how mistakes can ultimately lead to stronger bonds, greater empathy, and a deeper appreciation for the journey of motherhood. This activity encourages you to embrace vulnerability and honesty, allowing for an open dialogue about the complexities of parenting. Together, let's transform our perceived failures into powerful lessons that can enhance our relationships with our children and ourselves.

MISTAKES HAPPEN

Take a moment to identify a parenting mistake you have made. It can be anything you may wish you had done or said differently.

The Mistake

What did you learn from the experience?

MISTAKES HAPPEN

What did your children learn from the experience?

How did this impact your relationship with your children?

CELEBRA
your mista
it means
you'
Learnin

To the Office We Go, with Strollers in Tow

Understanding our unique path as professional women with children is a journey filled with opportunities for growth and transformation. As a parent and a professional, the intricate balance of nurturing our children while advancing our career can often feel overwhelming. However, this dual role can become the catalyst for profound personal development. My experiences as a systems thinker, administrator, and a researcher offers a unique perspective on challenges, one that can inspire not only my children but also my community. It was truly the COVID pandemic and all of the changes occurring during that period that forced me to take a step back and refine my approach to not only motherhood but to life, prior to charting forward.

I remember the moment as if it were yesterday: my boss held a college meeting and declared, "Business as usual." From his perspective, we were already teaching online and working from home, so the transition seemed seamless. However, for a select few of us, especially those household matriarchs with small children, the reality was far more complicated. With all schools closed, the added responsibility of parenting around the clock presented an entirely new layer of nuance. My father and spiritual guide had recently passed away. I had just relocated to a new area, and my spouse had decided to leave the relationship and remain hours away from the new home. Suddenly, I found myself not just a professional and a mother but also a full-time homeschool teacher, navigating the challenges of development and learning for my children for what felt like an eternity—18 months. Isolation and overwhelm were just the tip of the iceberg of what I was going through.

During this tumultuous time, my additional "moonlighting" role as a research administrator for an emotional intelligence grant within a local school district also came to an end. Balancing my career ambitions with the demands of motherhood was becoming far less straightforward than it seemed in the past. I quickly realized that the notion of "business as usual" was an unrealistic expectation for my situation. The upheaval in my personal life, coupled with the abrupt changes in my professional landscape, created an undeniable sense of disorientation and dissociation.

I found myself facing the daunting challenge of juggling work commitments while ensuring that my children received the age-appropriate attention and education they needed, all within the confines of our home. Adding to the complexity were the significant age gaps among my children: a newborn, a toddler, an elementary school student, and the eldest navigating the early stages of middle school. Each of their unique needs required careful consideration, making the task of balancing it all even more demanding.

As the weight of chaos continued to attempt to smother and ground me, I made a conscious choice to prioritize my children. This realization led me to actively reshape my career, via determination to find a path that truly reflected who I am and what fulfills me. I didn't give up on my professional aspirations; instead, I reenvisioned them to align with my family's needs and my children's development. This meant writing fewer research papers and turning my focus toward creating children's books that would engage young minds. I also developed a homeschool curriculum that allowed me to teach all my children the same topic, tailored to their individual levels, fostering a cohesive learning environment. Additionally, I founded a youth outreach program called "Systems at Any Age," aimed at introducing children, parents, and communities to the principles of systems thinking and empowerment. By making these intentional choices, I infused my career with purpose and meaning, ensuring that my work not only supported my professional growth but also enriched my children's lives and learning experiences.

This decision wasn't made lightly; it required deep reflection and an hone assessment of my changing circumstances. I realized that, while my career he importance, both myself and my children's emotional and educational nee were paramount, especially during such an unprecedented time. Prioritizing th not only helped me navigate that chaotic period but also gave me the streng to face future challenges with intention. In choosing my children, I four renewed purpose and resilience, transforming a difficult situation into profound opportunity for connection and growth.

Still today, raising four school-age children brings added complexity to an already demanding life. Each day introduces a fresh array of responsibilities, from helping my children navigate their responsibilities to fostering relationships with their schools and other parents and service providers during afterschool activities. I've come to appreciate the value of embracing this chaos as a series of invaluable experiences that profoundly shape my identity.

What's even more notable is what I learned about the importance of acknowledging that our professional background irrespective of each unique discipline, equips us with invaluable skills, which we can apply to parenting and vice versa.

In our next activity, we will utilize a Venn diagram to explore and reflect on the skills you have acquired as a mother and as a professional. This visual tool will help you identify the unique competencies gained in each role, as well as the overlapping skills that enrich both aspects of your life. As you fill in the diagram, consider how your experiences in motherhood- such as patience, multitasking, and emotional intelligence- intersect with your professional skills like leadership, problem-solving, and effective communication. Afterward, you will reflect on how these dual roles positively influence each other, enhancing your effectiveness in both areas. By recognizing the synergies between your personal and professional growth, you can gain a deeper appreciation for the multifaceted nature of your identity and the strengths you bring to both your family and your career.

As we navigate these roles, it's essential to recognize the lessons our children teach us as well. They provide a fresh perspective on creativity, resilience, and joy. They are also at the forefront of many of the technology shifts and social systems we are watching evolve and possibly less enthused about partaking in. Each moment spent with our children is an opportunity to reflect on our own values and priorities. By intentionally engaging with them, we not only nurture their growth but also allow our professional aspirations to flourish. This symbiotic relationship can lead to innovative ideas and approaches in both our personal and professional life. Their unfiltered view of the world can challenge our assumptions and inspire us to think differently, ultimately enriching both our lives and theirs. Thus, investing in their development is not just about shaping their future; it's about shaping our own, too.

RECOGNIZING INTERSECTION

Take a moment to acknowledge the skills and qualities of both your role as a mother and a professional. Are some skills distinctively unique? Are there skills that these roles share?

Skillful Mother

Skillful Professional

How does these roles positively influence each other?

Our journey, with all its complexities, can inspire others to embrace their own dual roles. Sharing our experiences, the highs and the lows, empowers fellow parents and professionals to navigate their own paths. By being honest about the challenges we face, we create a supportive community where everyone feels encouraged to pursue their passions while managing family life. This authenticity cultivates understanding and compassion, allowing each of us to lead by example and inspire those in our circles.

Hence, understanding our unique path is about embracing the duality of our existence as a parent and a professional. It is an opportunity to harness our experiences, skills, and insights to cultivate a fulfilling life. By viewing our journey through the lens of intentionality, we can transform challenges into growth opportunities, enriching not only our own life but also the lives of our children and those we encounter in our professional sphere. Every step we take on this path is a testament to the power of resilience, creativity, and passion.

Family Engagement Opportunity

Imperfect Art

Encourage each family member to create a piece of art without striving for perfection. Allow for experimentation, mistakes, and unexpected outcomes. The focus should be on the process of creation and expressing individuality, not on achieving a flawless result.

Chapter 3:
The Power of Intentionality

"Discipline is choosing between what you want now
and what you want most."

— Abraham Lincoln

Defining Intentional Motherhood

Intentional motherhood is a conscious approach to parenting that goes beyond mere survival. It is about embracing the profound responsibilities that come with raising a child while infusing each moment with purpose and thoughtfulness. This definition transcends the traditional notions of motherhood, inviting mothers to be active participants in our children's development rather than passive observers. By adopting this mindset, we can build a nurturing environment where both mothers and our children can thrive. It reflects a commitment to growth, both for the parent and the child, acknowledging that every challenge can serve as an agent for greater understanding and connection.

At its core, intentional motherhood encompasses the idea of mindfulness in parenting. This means being fully present in each interaction, whether it's during a mundane morning routine or a teachable moment in the middle of a playground visit. It requires a keen awareness of one's values and goals, allowing us to make decisions that align with our vision for our family. When we practice mindfulness, we cultivate patience and empathy, which are essential ingredients for fostering strong relationships with our children. This intentional presence can transform everyday challenges into opportunities for learning and growth, both for the parent and the child.

Moreover, intentional motherhood recognizes the importance of self-care and personal development. A mother who is committed to her own growth is better equipped to nurture her children. By prioritizing our well-being, we model for our children the value of self-love and personal responsibility. This journey of self-discovery enables us to identify our strengths and weaknesses, paving the way for authentic connections with our children. It encourages us to pursue our passions and interests, reminding us that we are not solely defined by our role as a parent but as individuals with dreams and aspirations.

In the next activity, we will explore what mindfulness in parenting means to you and examine the challenges you encounter in being fully present during your daily activities.

BE MINDFUL

Self-Reflection:

What does mindfulness in parenting mean to you? What challenges do you face in being fully present? Think of a single way you may be able to cultivate greater mindfulness in your daily interactions with your children.

Intentional motherhood also emphasizes the significance of community and support. No mother should navigate the complexities of parenting in isolation. Building connections with other mothers, mentors, and professionals creates a network of support that can be invaluable during challenging times. By sharing experiences and insights, we can inspire one another and collectively redefine what it means to be intentional in our parenting. This sense of belonging not only enhances personal growth but also enriches the lives of children by exposing them to varied perspectives and experiences.

Ultimately, defining intentional motherhood is about embracing a mindset that celebrates both the challenges and joys of parenting. It is a commitment to nurturing not just children, but also oneself, cultivating a legacy of growth, resilience, and love. This journey is not always easy, but by consciously choosing to approach motherhood with intention, we can transform obstacles into valuable lessons. As we navigate the complexities of parenting, we will find that intentional motherhood is a powerful catalyst for personal and familial transformation, leading to a richer, more fulfilling life for everyone involved.

Setting Intentional Goals for Yourself and Your Family

Setting intentional goals is a powerful way for parents and families to create a clear path toward growth and fulfillment. It begins with a deep understanding of our values and aspirations. As you reflect on what truly matters to you and your family, you can establish goals that resonate with your core beliefs. This alignment ensures that the journey toward these goals is not only productive but also enriching. When our family members share a vision, we create a supportive environment that nurtures individual strengths while fostering unity.

In the hustle and bustle of daily life, it's easy to drift away from what we truly desire. Intentional goal setting invites us to take a step back, assess our current situation, and envision where we want to go. This process involves open conversations with our family, encouraging everyone to share their dreams and ambitions. By involving each family member, we cultivate a sense of ownership and commitment to the collective goals. This collaboration not only strengthens family bonds but also empowers each individual to pursue their unique aspirations within a supportive framework.

The family engagement activities at the end of this chapter are designed to help your family work on collective aims. Once you have identified your family's goals, it's essential to break them down into manageable steps. This approach transforms daunting aspirations into achievable milestones, making the journey less overwhelming. Each small victory fuels motivation and reinforces the importance of perseverance. Encourage your family to celebrate these milestones, no matter how minor they may seem. Celebrating progress together fosters a culture of appreciation and resilience, reminding everyone that growth is a continuous process filled with learning opportunities.

In our next activity, we will focus on brainstorming meaningful ways for your family to celebrate the achievements of your collective goals, no matter how big or small. This is an opportunity to reflect on the moments that matter and to think creatively about how to honor those achievements together. Remember that the scale of the celebration is far less important than the significance of the act itself; it's about creating shared experiences that foster connection and joy. Whether it's a simple family outing, a movie night at home, or a special dinner where everyone shares what they're proud of, these moments can strengthen your family bond and reinforce the importance of supporting one another. Let's use this activity to generate ideas that resonate with your family's unique dynamics and values, ensuring that each celebration reflects the love and commitment you share in reaching your goals.

Remember that as you set and pursue your goals, it's vital to remain flexible and adaptable. Life is unpredictable, and circumstances may shift, requiring you to reassess your goals periodically. This adaptability is not a sign of failure but rather an opportunity for growth. Regular family meetings to review your progress, discuss challenges, and adjust goals as necessary can create a dynamic environment of support. In this way, your family can navigate life's unpredictability while maintaining a shared vision for the future. setting intentional goals is not just about achieving outcomes; it's about fostering a mindset of growth, resilience, and unity within your families. When you embark on this journey together, you create an atmosphere where everyone feels valued and inspired. By nurturing each other's dreams and supporting one another in overcoming challenges, you lay the foundation for a thriving family dynamic. Embrace this transformative process, and watch as you collectively rise to new heights, turning challenges into opportunities for growth and connection.

CELEBRATING TOGETHER

Take some time to brainstorm creative ways to celebrate your family's shared achievements, both big and small. Consider a variety of activities that you can enjoy together, whether at home or out in the community. Think about celebrations of different scales—ranging from simple, intimate gestures to larger gatherings or outings—that will honor your accomplishments and strengthen your family bonds.

Idea

Idea

Idea

Idea

Idea

Idea

"Family is not an important thing. It's everything."
- Michael J. Fox

Discipline, Boundaries, Structure and Control

Discipline, boundaries, structure, and control are often viewed as rigid concepts, but in reality, they form the core of a nurturing environment for both parents and children. As I reflected on my journey, I realized that I never truly appreciated their significance until I found myself grappling with the chaos of not doing so. The days blurred together, and I often felt like a ship adrift at sea, lacking the anchor that discipline and structure provide. In those moments of uncertainty, I began to understand that these elements are not merely rules to follow, but vital components that foster growth and development within families.

Creating discipline and structure in our homes require intentional effort and a commitment to consistency. It is easy to fall into the trap of reacting to daily challenges without a clear plan. However, setting boundaries creates a sense of safety and predictability for our children. They thrive in environments where they understand expectations and feel secure. By establishing routines and guidelines, we not only empower our children to make better choices but also cultivate a sense of responsibility within ourselves. This realization can be a significant turning point; thus, discipline is an act of love, providing the framework for our children to flourish.

As we navigate the complexities of motherhood, it is pertinent to understand that boundaries are not about control but rather about creating a space for healthy relationships. When we struggle to define these boundaries, we may often feel overwhelmed, leading to frustration and confusion for both our children and ourselves. However, by embracing the idea that boundaries are essential for mutual respect, we will also begin to communicate more effectively. Learning to express our needs and expectations clearly, will in turn allow our children to understand their roles within our family unit. This clarity fosters trust and encourages open dialogue, transforming interactions into opportunities for growth.

In the next activity, you will consider a series of "What Would You Do?" scenarios aimed at examining effective strategies for managing boundaries and discipline with your children. I reference related, grounded theories to honor the researcher within me and to provide keywords or terminology for additional knowledge development.

INTENTIONAL BOUNDARIES

What Would You Do (WWYD)?

It's 8:30 PM, and 6-year-old Alexis is supposed to be in bed. She's stalling, asking for "just one more story" and then another, and generally resisting going to sleep.

2 CONSIDER ALTERNATIVES

WWYD: Which of the following do you think is the most effective way to handle this situation?

a) "Alexis, it's past your bedtime. Two more stories, and then it's lights out." (This approach acknowledges her desire for stories while setting a clear limit.)

b) "Fine, stay up all night. I'm going to bed." (This is dismissive and may escalate the power struggle.)

c) "If you don't go to bed right now, there will be no TV tomorrow." (This focuses on punishment rather than clear expectations.)

d) "Okay, one more story, but then it's lights out, no exceptions." (This sets a clear boundary with a small compromise.)

3 GROUNDED IN THEORY

This scenario highlights the importance of clear and consistent expectations (from Behavioral Psychology). Setting a predictable routine helps children feel secure and reduces power struggles.

INTENTIONAL BOUNDARIES

What Would You Do (WWYD)?

1 SCENARIO 2

> 3-year-old Bryce has a new toy truck, and his older sister, 5-year-old Erica, wants to play with it. Bryce starts to cry and refuses to share.

2 CONSIDER ALTERNATIVES

WWYD: Which of the following do you think is the most effective way to handle this situation?

a) "Erica, you've been playing with his toys all day. It's his turn to play with his own toys." (This acknowledges Bryce's feelings and prioritizes his ownership.)

b) "Bryce, you need to learn to share. Erica can play with your truck for a little while." (This may not consider Bryce's feelings and could lead to resentment.)

c) "Let's find another toy for Erica to play with. How about your dolls?" (This offers a solution while respecting Bryce's feelings.)

d) "If you don't share, you'll lose your truck." (This focuses on punishment and may not teach valuable social skills.)

3 GROUNDED IN THEORY

This scenario touches upon Social Learning Theory, which emphasizes the importance of modeling and observational learning. By observing how the mother handles conflict, children learn how to resolve disputes and develop empathy.

INTENTIONAL BOUNDARIES

What Would You Do (WWYD)?

1 **SCENARIO 3**

> 10-year-old Shawn has exceeded his agreed-upon screen time limit. He argues that he needs to finish a level in his video game.

2 **CONSIDER ALTERNATIVES**

WWYD: Which of the following do you think is the most effective way to handle this situation?

a) "I don't care about your game. You've used up your time." (This is dismissive and ignores his feelings.)

b) "Okay, you can finish this level, but then the game is off." (This offers a small compromise while upholding the limit.)

c) "Let's negotiate. You can finish this level, but you have to read for 30 minutes afterward." (This encourages negotiation and responsibility.)

d) "No screens for the rest of the day." (This may be too severe and can lead to resentment.)

3 **GROUNDED IN THEORY**

This scenario relates to Self-Determination Theory, which emphasizes the importance of autonomy and choice in fostering intrinsic motivation. Allowing children some input in setting limits can increase their buy-in and cooperation.

INTENTIONAL BOUNDARIES

What Would You Do (WWYD)?

SCENARIO 4

> 8-year-old twins, Tomas and Sophie, are constantly arguing and fighting over toys and attention.

2 CONSIDER ALTERNATIVES

WWYD: Which of the following do you think is the most effective way to handle this situation?

a) "If you two don't stop fighting, I'm taking away all your toys." (This is a blanket punishment that may not effectively address the underlying issues.)

b) "I can see you're both upset. Let's try to find a way to solve this problem together." (This encourages problem-solving and conflict resolution skills.)

c) "Sophie, you're always starting the arguments. Go to your room." (This may unfairly blame one child and escalate the conflict.)

d) "I'm not going to listen to your arguing anymore. Go play somewhere else." (This avoids the issue and may not help the children learn to resolve conflicts.)

3 GROUNDED IN THEORY

This scenario emphasizes the importance of teaching children effective conflict resolution strategies, such as active listening, empathy, and negotiation. These skills are crucial for healthy social and emotional development.

INTENTIONAL BOUNDARIES

What Would You Do (WWYD)?

 SCENARIO 5

> 4-year-old Mya is having a tantrum in the grocery store, screaming and kicking because she wants a candy bar.

 CONSIDER ALTERNATIVES

WWYD: Which of the following do you think is the most effective way to handle this situation?

a) "I understand you're upset, but we're not buying candy today. Let's go find some fruit." (This acknowledges her feelings while setting a firm boundary.)

b) "Stop this right now! You're embarrassing me!" (This is dismissive and may escalate the tantrum.)

c) "Okay, we'll buy the candy if you stop crying." (This rewards the negative behavior.)

d) Ignore her and keep shopping. She'll stop eventually. (This may not address her needs and could reinforce the tantrum behavior.)

GROUNDED IN THEORY

This scenario highlights the importance of emotional regulation and impulse control. By helping children learn to manage their emotions in challenging situations, parents can equip them with valuable life skills.

These scenarios, while simple in their presentation, highlight universally relatable behaviors and conflicts that transcend specific ages and situations. They help us reflect on common parenting challenges and encourage thoughtful discussions about establishing healthy limits while fostering a positive environment for growth and learning.

The journey of establishing structure and control is not without its challenges. There will likely be moments of setback and doubt, where we question our ability to maintain the discipline we seek to instill. Yet, it is through these struggles that we will discover the power of resilience. Each time we revisit our family values and reaffirm our goals, we will find renewed strength. It is evident that creating structure is a dynamic process; it evolves as we do. By embracing flexibility within your framework, you will also learn to adapt to the changing needs of your children, reinforcing the idea that discipline does not mean rigidity.

In our next activity, we will take a thoughtful look at the distinction between discipline and punishment, exploring the philosophy behind each approach and the impact they can have on your child's development. You will consider whether there are circumstances where punishment may be appropriate, or if discipline should always be the guiding principle in our parenting. Through this reflection, you will have the opportunity to identify one specific way you can employ discipline to teach and guide your child effectively, using a concrete example from your own experiences. By understanding the nuances between these concepts, you can cultivate a parenting style that emphasizes teaching and growth, ultimately fostering a more positive and constructive relationship with your child.

In summary, the path to finding discipline, boundaries, structure, and control is a journey steeped in personal growth. For me, the key has been to appreciate that these elements are not burdens but gifts that enable us to guide our children towards independence and success. The intentional creation of these frameworks will transform both your parenting and your perspective on motherhood. As we continue to navigate the challenges ahead, hold fast to the belief that with discipline and intentionality, we can turn obstacles into opportunities for growth, nurturing a legacy of resilience and strength within our family.

CONSEQUENCES

Self-Reflection:

Reflect on the differences between discipline and punishment, recognizing that they serve distinct purposes in parenting. Are there situations where you believe punishment may be more appropriate than discipline? Consider this carefully. Additionally, brainstorm at least one specific strategy you can employ to use discipline as a means to teach and guide your child, focusing on how this approach can address misbehavior while fostering learning and growth.

Family Engagement Opportunity

Family Vision Board

Collaboratively create a vision board that encapsulates your family's shared goals, serving as a visual reminder to keep everyone motivated and focused on your collective aspirations.

Family Rules

Gather together with your children and other household members to collaboratively brainstorm a set of family rules. This inclusive process not only fosters a sense of ownership among the children but also increases their commitment to following the rules.

Chapter 4:
Systems Thinking in Motherhood

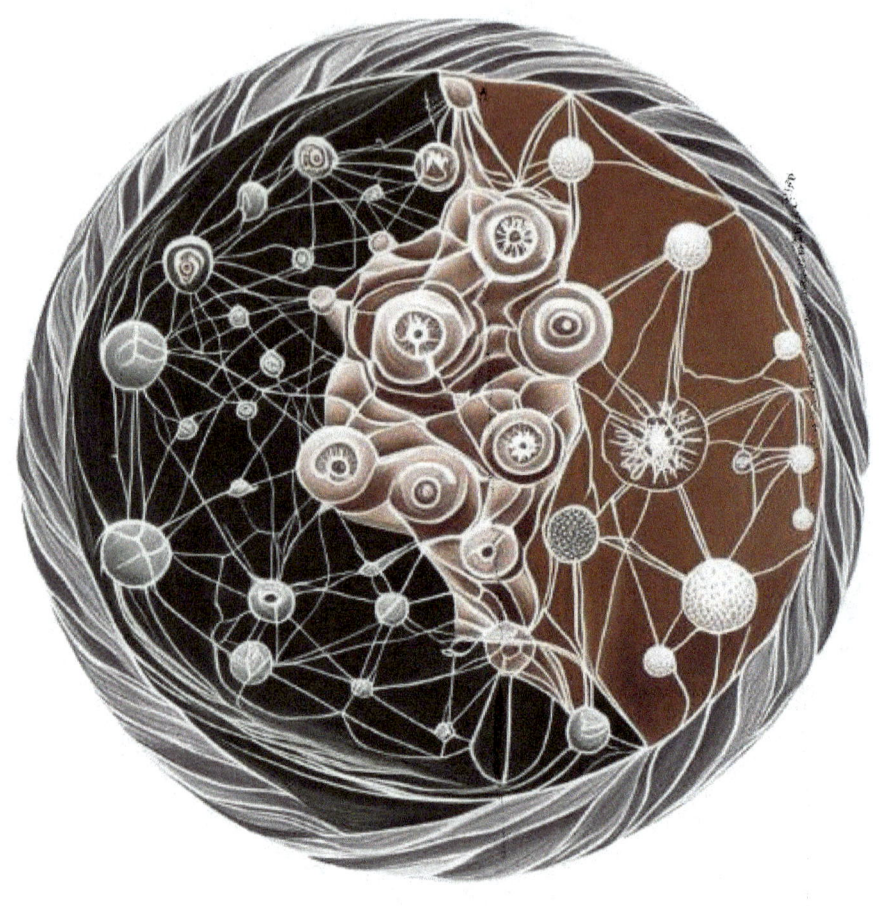

"The system, to a large extent, causes its own behavior!"
— Peter Senge

Intentional Motherhood and Systems Thinking

As a systems engineer, I have always been drawn to the idea that most aspects of life can be understood as interconnected systems—where individual elements come together to form a cohesive whole. Throughout my lifetime, I have spent countless hours making connections and applying systems thinking, often without even realizing it. This perspective has shaped not only my professional endeavors but also my personal experiences, including my journey as a mother. Recognizing the intricate relationships and dynamics that underpin the art of parenting, I felt compelled to dedicate a section of this book to exploring intentional motherhood through the lens of systems thinking. By doing so, I hope to illuminate how understanding these connections can empower mothers to navigate their roles with purpose and clarity, ultimately fostering healthier family systems and nurturing environments for their children.

Intentional motherhood is indeed a concept that encapsulates the deliberate and thoughtful approach to parenting, recognizing the profound impact that maternal choices have on the child, family, and broader societal systems. Think about how each of the 14 Areas of Systems Thinking (ASTS) might show up in your own family dynamics as you read through this chapter – you'll have an opportunity to explore these connections further in an upcoming activity. Keep in mind that this chapter intends to explore how these ASTS can illuminate the intricacies of intentional motherhood and enhance our understanding of parenting as a dynamic system.

ASTS: Multiple Perspectives
(Translation: Think in Different Ways)

Intentional motherhood requires an appreciation of multiple perspectives, recognizing that motherhood is experienced differently across various cultures, socioeconomic backgrounds, and personal circumstances. For instance, a mother's approach may differ significantly based on her professional background, educational level, or community support systems. By engaging various stakeholders—partners, family members, educators, and community leaders—mothers can draw on rich insights, ensuring that their parenting strategies are well- rounded and informed by diverse viewpoints.

ASTS: Different Scales of Abstraction
(Translation: Separate into Parts and Put it Together)

Motherhood operates at various levels of abstraction, from the micro-level interactions between mother and child to the macro-level implications of parenting styles on societal norms and policies. Understanding these scales allows mothers to navigate their roles more effectively. For example, a mother may focus on day-to-day nurturing while also advocating for policy changes that support parental leave or childcare resources, recognizing how her actions at both levels can influence broader systems.

ASTS: Interconnections, Intrarelationships, and Dependencies
(Translation: Explore Things that are Closely Connected)

The relationships between mothers, their children, and their environment are complex and interconnected. Mothers often rely on support networks, including family, friends, and community resources. Recognizing these dependencies helps mothers understand how their well-being influences their children's development and vice versa. This interconnectedness emphasizes the importance of community support in fostering healthy family dynamics.

ASTS: Dynamic Behavior
(Translation: Consider What it Does and Could Do)

The responses of mothers and children are not static but dynamic, influenced by vario factors such as emotional states, environmental changes, and social pressures, especially this era of social media. For example, a child's behavior may change in response stressors in the home or community, prompting a mother to adapt her parenti strategies. The constant exposure to idealized lifestyles and trending content on soc media can impact a child's self-esteem and create new social pressures, requiring mothe to navigate these digital influences. By observing these dynamics, mothers can bett understand emergent behaviors and adjust their approaches to meet their childre evolving needs.

ASTS: Stock, Flow, and Delay
(Translation: Understand What is Needed, Used and the Time Required to Realize Change)

This ASTS element highlights the resources a mother manages—time, energy, emotional bandwidth, and financial assets. Intentional motherhood involves recognizing the "stock" of resources available and the "flow" of these resources in response to the demands of parenting. For instance, a mother's ability to allocate time for self-care can directly impact her parenting effectiveness. Understanding delays in the impact of these resources, such as the long-term effects of stress on children's development, is crucial for intentional decision-making.

ASTS: Feedback
(Translation: Monitor the Effects of Different Actions)

Feedback loops are integral to intentional motherhood. A mother's actions can create both positive and negative feedback. For example, responsive parenting can enhance a child's emotional security, while punitive measures may lead to behavioral issues. A positive feedback loop might involve a mother consistently encouraging her child's curiosity, which leads the child to become a lifelong learner, further fueling their intellectual growth. A negative feedback loop could be a mother's anxiety about her child's performance leading to excessive pressure, which in turn causes the child to become anxious and underperform, reinforcing the mother's initial anxiety. Understanding these feedback mechanisms allows mothers to refine their approaches continuously, fostering healthier relationships and promoting positive outcomes.

ASTS: Non-linear Relationships
(Translation: Discover How Things are Connected at a Broader Level)

The relationships involved in motherhood are often non-linear, characterized by unexpected outcomes and complex interactions. For instance, a mother's decision to pursue a career while parenting may yield unforeseen consequences, such as increased resilience in her child or challenges related to work-life balance. Similarly, a mother might initially believe that strict routines are essential for raising well-behaved children, only to discover that a more flexible approach fosters greater creativity and independence in her child. Or a mother's well-intentioned efforts to protect her child from disappointment might inadvertently lead to a child who struggles with resilience and coping skills later on. Despite the specific example, embracing non-linearity encourages mothers to remain adaptable and open to change, recognizing that parenting does not follow a predictable path.

ASTS: Mental and Formal Models
(Translation: Examine What you Think you Know and What you Need to Know)

Mothers often navigate their roles using both mental and formal models of parenting. These models are shaped by personal experiences, cultural narratives, and societal expectations. A mother might have a mental model of family meals as a time for connection, shaped by her own childhood. Or a mother might consciously choose to move away from a mental model of authoritarian parenting, based on her own negative experiences, and instead adopt a formal model of gentle parenting, seeking out resources and support to implement it effectively. By becoming aware of these models, mothers can critically assess their beliefs and behaviors, identifying areas for growth and adaptation. This self-awareness is key to intentional motherhood, as it empowers mothers to align their practices with their values and goals.

ASTS: System Structure and Boundary
(Translation: Realize What it is and What it is Not)

Understanding the structure and boundaries of the family system is essential for intentional motherhood. Mothers must consider what elements define their family unit, including roles, responsibilities, and external influences. For example, a family might establish a clear boundary around homework time, designating a specific space and time free from distractions, where parents are available to offer support but the child is primarily responsible for completing their assignments. Imagine a family where extended family members frequently offer unsolicited advice on parenting; the parents might establish a boundary by politely but firmly communicating their chosen parenting style and requesting that advice be offered only when explicitly asked for. Setting clear boundaries can protect family dynamics from external pressures, such as societal expectations or economic challenges, enabling mothers to cultivate a nurturing environment.

ASTS: Conceptual Modeling
(Translation: Make it Easier to See and Understand)

Mothers can benefit from conceptual modeling to visualize their parenting strategies and the relationships between various elements in their lives. By mapping out their goals, challenges, and resources, mothers can create a clearer picture of their parenting landscape, facilitating more informed decision-making and planning. For example, a mother struggling with work-life balance might create a conceptual model that visually represents her work commitments, family responsibilities, personal needs, and available support systems. This model could help her identify potential conflicts, prioritize tasks, and explore solutions like adjusting her work schedule or seeking childcare assistance. As an additional example, a mother whose child is struggling with anxiety might create a conceptual model that connects her child's triggers, emotional responses, coping mechanisms, and available support resources, such as therapy or mindfulness exercises. This model could help her better understand the interplay of these factors and develop a more targeted approach to supporting her child.

ASTS: Prospection and Prediction
(Translation: Predict What May Happen Next or Over Time)

Intentional motherhood requires the ability to anticipate the long-term impacts of parenting decisions. Mothers can develop foresight by reflecting on their choices and considering how these may affect their children's futures. For instance, investing in a child's education today can have profound implications for their career opportunities tomorrow. A mother who encourages her child's curiosity and fosters a love of learning is not only setting them up for academic success but also cultivating a lifelong passion that will enrich their lives. Similarly, a mother who models healthy emotional regulation is likely to raise children who are better equipped to manage their own emotions and build strong relationships.

ASTS: Hypothetical and Inferential Considerations
(Translation: Gather Useful Clues from Other Things)

Intentional motherhood often involves engaging in hypothetical and inferential thinking. Mothers must consider various scenarios and outcomes based on their decisions, drawing insights from multiple disciplines such as psychology, education, and sociology. For example, a mother might hypothesize about the effects of different disciplinary approaches—such as positive reinforcement versus punitive measures—on her child's behavior and emotional development. By analyzing the implications of these hypothetical situations, mothers can make more informed choices that align with their parenting philosophy.

ASTS 13: Paradoxical and Ambiguity Tolerance
(Translation: Accept That All the Information May Not be Available)

Motherhood is often rife with paradoxes and ambiguity. Mothers may find themselves navigating conflicting advice, societal pressures, and their own desires. For instance, the tension between pursuing a career and being present for their children can create feelings of guilt and uncertainty. Tolerance for these paradoxes allows mothers to embrace the complexities of their role without being overwhelmed by them.

ASTS 14: Creativity
(Translation: Brainstorm or Improve Ideas and Alternatives)

Creativity plays a vital role in intentional motherhood. Mothers are often required to think outside the box to address the diverse needs of their children and families. Whether it's devising unique solutions for educational challenges, finding new ways to connect with their children, or managing household dynamics, creativity empowers mothers to innovate and improve their parenting practices.

Having provided you with a "firehose" overview of systems thinking, the next activity is designed to deepen your understanding of the interconnectedness of your experiences and to help you actively apply systems thinking principles within your unique motherhood journey.

AREAS OF SYSTEMS THINKING SKILLS

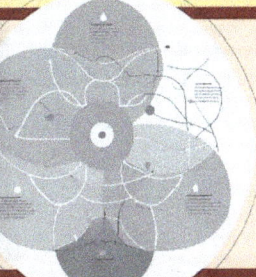

Take a moment to think about your own motherhood journey and identify a meaningful example that illustrates each of the 14 Areas of Systems Thinking (ASTS). Consider how these principles have manifested in your experiences, decisions, and relationships as a mother.

Multiple Perspectives

Different Scales of Abstraction

Interconnections, Intra-relationships and Dependencies

Dynamic Behavior

Stock, Flow, and Delay

Feedback

Non-Linear Relationships	Mental and Formal Models
System Structure & Boundaries	**Conceptual Modeling**
Prospection & Prediction	**Hypothetical & Inferential Consideration**
Paradoxical & Ambiguity Tolerance	**Creativity**

Integrating Intentional Motherhood and Systems Thinking

The intersection of intentional motherhood and the ASTS framework provides a comprehensive lens through which to understand the complexities of parenting. By applying systems thinking principles, mothers can navigate their roles with greater awareness and intentionality, recognizing the interconnectedness of their choices, relationships, and environments.

As mothers engage with the 14 ASTS as a way of thinking about their family, they cultivate a deeper understanding of their parenting systems, empowering them to make informed decisions that positively impact their children's development and well-being. This holistic approach not only enriches the experience of motherhood but also contributes to the creation of healthier family units and, by extension, stronger communities.

The following self-reflection activity invites you to explore your motherhood journey through the lens of systems thinking, recognizing the intricate web of interconnectedness that shapes your relationships, decisions and dynamics. Consider how your actions ripple through your family system, impacting not only your children but also your partner, extended family, and even yourself. You will be challenged to identify one specific relationship within your family that you would like to nurture and strengthen. Then, brainstorm a practical, actionable step you can take to foster that connection and improve its dynamic.

Essentially, in embracing the principles of systems thinking, intentional motherhood evolves into a dynamic, responsive practice that acknowledges the multifaceted nature of parenting. By recognizing the complexities and interdependencies within their systems, mothers can foster resilience not only in themselves but also in their children, preparing them to thrive in an ever-changing world.

SYSTEMS THINKING

Self-Reflection:

Reflect on your journey as a mother through the lens of systems thinking. Consider the various elements that contribute to your family system—your relationships with your children, partner, extended family, and community. How do these interconnections influence your parenting choices and the overall dynamics of your family? Identify one specific relationship or connection that you would like to strengthen and outline a practical step you can take to nurture that bond.

Family Engagement Opportunity

Family Systems Map

Explore the topic of systems thinking as a family. Discuss how every family is a system made up of different members (elements) and the relationships between them. Expand the map by adding other important elements of the family system, such as pets, shared activities (like family game nights), or outside influences (school, friends, activities). Draw connections between these elements and family members to illustrate how they impact one another.

Chapter 5:
From Challenge to Opportunity

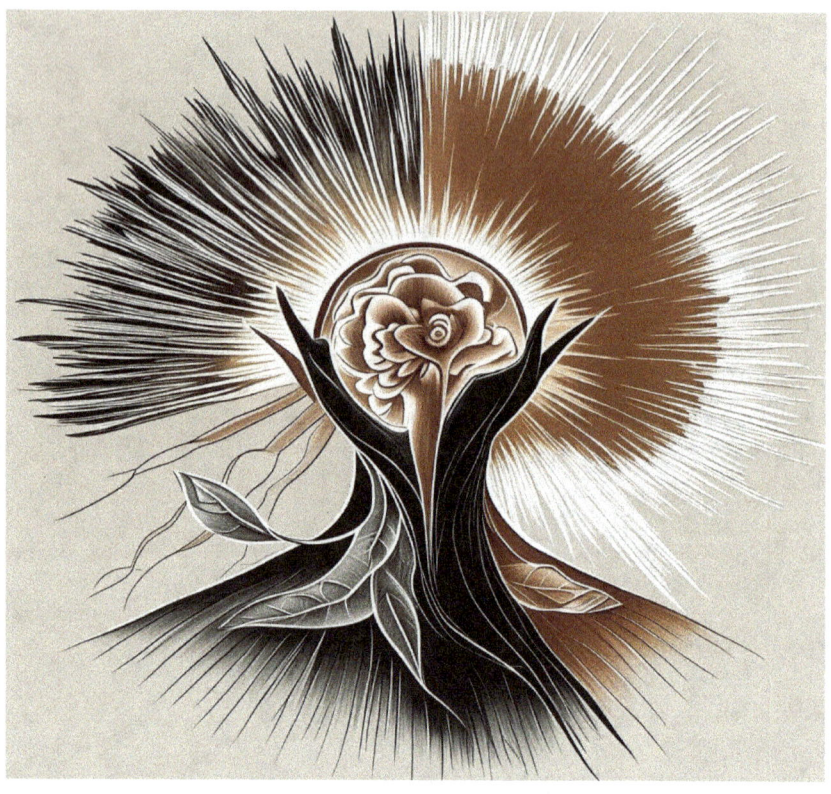

"The greatest glory in living lies not in never falling, but in rising every time we fall."

— Nelson Mandela

Common Parenting Challenges

In the whirlwind of parenting, particularly when we have multiple children, the unexpected often becomes part of the daily routine. Emergencies and unplanned needs can arise at any moment, demanding immediate attention and quick decision-making. As mothers, we often find ourselves in the role of the rescuer, responding to our children's needs with unwavering dedication. However, this constant state of readiness can lead to an accumulation of sacrifices that weigh heavily on our mental health. Recognizing this pattern is the first step toward reclaiming our well-being and transforming these challenges into growth opportunities.

The diverse stages of childhood and adolescence present unique challenges too, especially when juggling the needs of four children at different developmental phases and genders. From navigating early childhood education to managing high school pressures, each child requires tailored support and attention. This variability can create a sense of hypervisibility at work, where unplanned emergencies may pull us away from our professional obligations. While it may be a reality I must accept in the moment, it also underscores a deeper challenge that requires me to actively seek mitigation strategies and support. It became essential to communicate these challenges openly with employers and colleagues, to cultivate an environment of understanding and flexibility that acknowledges the realities of parenthood.

Another example comes from what I term as being the "rideshare queen" of the family. Driving for hours each day, and in my case about 4 hours on average, to ensure that my children reach their destinations—be it school, extracurricular activities, or playdates—can be both rewarding and exhausting. Each trip is a testament to our love and commitment, but it can also drain our energy and leave little room for self-care. Embracing this role while acknowledging its toll on our mental health is crucial. It invites us to explore ways to balance our responsibilities with the need for personal time, fostering a healthier family dynamic.

As we embark on this next activity, you will focus on conducting a root cause analysis of a specific parenting challenge you are currently facing. Often, as parents, we become so caught up in the symptoms of a challenge that we overlook the underlying issues that contribute to our struggles. Whether it's a recurring conflict among your responsibilities, difficulty in managing your child's behavior, running out of time in the day, or challenges in maintaining healthier habits, it's easy to respond to the immediate concerns without addressing the core factors at play. This can lead to a cycle of temporary fixes that only provide relief in the short term, rather than fostering long-term solutions.

By taking the time to identify the root cause of your parenting challenges, you can gain valuable insights that will empower you to tackle the issue at its source. This approach encourages us to think critically about the dynamics within our family and consider how various factors—such as communication styles, expectations, or even external pressures— may be influencing the situation. Instead of merely putting out fires as they arise, we will explore the deeper motivations and circumstances that contribute to these challenges.

During this activity, you will choose one specific parenting challenge and analyze it through a structured framework commonly called the 5 Why's Method. You'll begin by describing the symptoms you observe and the immediate reactions that arise from them. Then, you will dig deeper to uncover the underlying causes, asking yourself probing questions that help illuminate the bigger picture.

Consider this scenario: your children are consistently late to school on Mondays (a challenge I'm still working on!). The surface issue might seem to be simple tiredness. But digging deeper—asking "why" repeatedly—can reveal the root cause. Perhaps the lack of a consistent weekend routine disrupts their sleep schedule. But *why* is the weekend different? Maybe, a I've realized in my own family, it's because certain tasks, like hair-doing, get pushed to the weekend instead of being incorporated into the weekday routine because of the amount o time and energy required. The solution, then, isn't just about Monday mornings; it's abou creating a more balanced rhythm throughout the entire week.

BUT Why?

Choose one parenting challenge you are currently experiencing.
Describe the nature of this challenge, and reflect on how it affects
you personally as well as its impact on your family dynamics.

CHALLENGE DESCRIPTION

PERSONAL IMPACT

FAMILY IMPACT

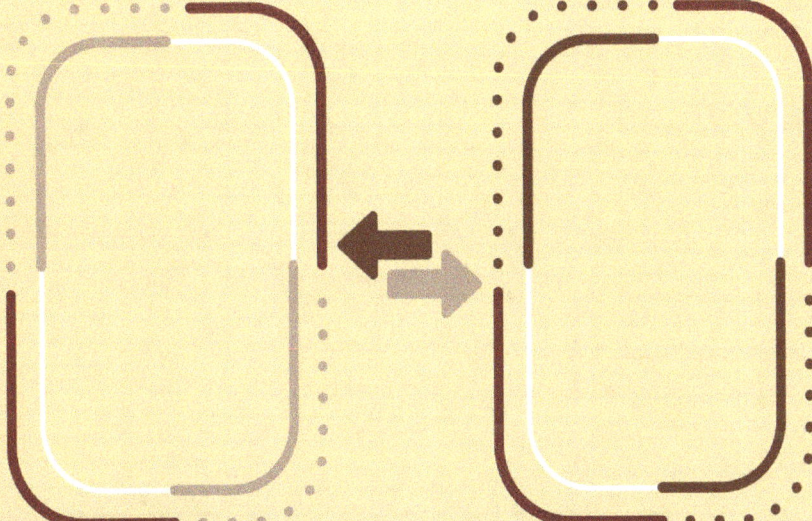

BUT Why?

Explore potential causes of the challenge and capture one of those causes. Use the 5 Why's method to uncover a root cause.

CAUSE

BUT WHY? _____

BUT WHY? _____

BUT WHY? _____

BUT WHY? _____

BUT WHY? _____

ROOT CAUSE >>>> _____

For the root cause, consider potential solutions or mitigation strategies to address the challenge.

SOLUTION

This reflective process not only aids in understanding the complexities of your parenting struggles but also sets the stage for implementing effective strategies that address the root issues, leading to more sustainable, positive changes in your family life. Let's take this opportunity to move beyond surface-level solutions and develop a more profound understanding of the challenges we face as parents.

In the midst of dynamic demands, it is vital to prioritize self-care and establish boundaries. As parents, we often place our needs last, but this can lead to burnout and resentment over time. By intentionally setting aside time for us—whether through quiet reflection, exercise, or pursuing hobbies—we can recharge our spirits and enhance our capacity to support our children. Implementing routines that include moments of respite not only benefits us but also models healthy habits for our children, teaching them the importance of balance in their own lives.

Ultimately, navigating the complexities of parenting requires resilience and adaptability. By recognizing and addressing the common challenges we face, we can transform them into opportunities for personal growth and family bonding. Embracing our roles with intention allows us to redefine what it means to be a parent in today's fast-paced world. It's a journey of learning, where we can inspire not only ourselves but also our children, cultivating a legacy of strength and self-awareness that will serve them well into their futures.

Reframing Challenges as Learning Experiences

Although parenting as a single person has not always been my circumstance, I am quickly approaching such reality as I recently entered the last phase of divorce and have been co- parenting across a distance of about 3 hours for the last 5 years. Given the impact of this newfound perspective on my journey, this book includes several nods to those navigating the complexities of divorce, co-parenting or an otherwise single parent dynamic. I understand there are many dynamics within the coupling of the term "co-parenting" each with their own insights and implications, but I will reference these relationships as "co-parenting" in this book for oversimplification and generalization.

While transitioning into such dynamics can feel overwhelming, it also presents a unique opportunity for personal growth and transformation. Each challenge faced during this time can be reframed as a learning experience that enriches not only our life but also the lives of our children. Approaching this journey with an open heart and a willingness to learn can turn difficult moments into tools for a more fulfilling and intentional motherhood. For me, this has not been an easy thing to learn or accept albeit ultimately an undeniable truth.

The emotional turbulence that often accompanies divorce or separation can serve as a powerful catalyst for self-discovery. As you confront feelings of loss, anger, or sadness, you are also prompted to explore your own values, beliefs, and aspirations. This introspection can lead to a deeper understanding of yourself, allowing you to emerge from the process with renewed strength and clarity. Embracing these emotions instead of suppressing them opens the door to resilience and self-compassion, essential qualities for both personal well-being and effective co-parenting.

Co-parenting introduces an entirely new dynamic that can be challenging but also rewarding. It requires a commitment to communication, collaboration, and compromise. By framing these challenges as growth opportunities, you can cultivate a more cooperative relationship with your ex-partner. This not only benefits you as you learn to navigate differences but also sets a positive example for your children. Teaching them the importance of empathy and understanding during conflicts will instill valuable life skills that they can carry into their own relationships.

In our next activity, I invite you to reflect on a significant change in your life that has impacted your parenting journey, whether it be a loss, relocation, divorce, or another transformative experience. Changes like these can profoundly affect not only your own emotional landscape but also the dynamics within your family. As you engage in this reflection, take time to consider what you have learned about yourself as you adapted to this change. How have your strengths and resilience emerged during this period of transition?

I encourage you to identify the positive aspects that may have arisen from this experience, whether it be newfound perspectives, deeper connections with your others, or personal growth that has enhanced your parenting or professional skills. Recognizing the silver linings in challenging situations can empower you and provide valuable insights into how you can continue to navigate future changes with grace and confidence. This activity aims to foster a deeper understanding of both your personal journey and the evolving nature of your role as a parent, thus enriching your family's experience as you move forward together.

Therefore, reframing the narrative around challenges empower us to transform what might seem like an ending into a vibrant new beginning. Each challenge is an opportunity to cultivate resilience, foster meaningful connections, and model intentional living for our children. By embracing this mindset, we can navigate any transition with confidence, knowing that we are not only shaping our own journey but also nurturing the emotional well-being of our children as they learn to adapt to evolving family dynamics.

LIFE HAPPENS

Self-Reflection:

Reflect on a significant life change that has impacted your parenting. What insights have you gained about yourself during this challenging period? Consider several positive outcomes that have emerged from this experience.

Family Engagement Opportunity

Challenge Jar

As a family, brainstorm a list of common challenges you face, now or in the past (e.g., homework struggles, sibling disagreements, frustration with a hobby, feeling overwhelmed). Write each challenge on a separate card. Place all the "Challenge Cards" in a jar. At any time, select and read a challenge and allow the family to identify something positive that came out of the past challenge and/or ideas for addressing the challenge.

Chapter 6:
Building a Resilient Mindset

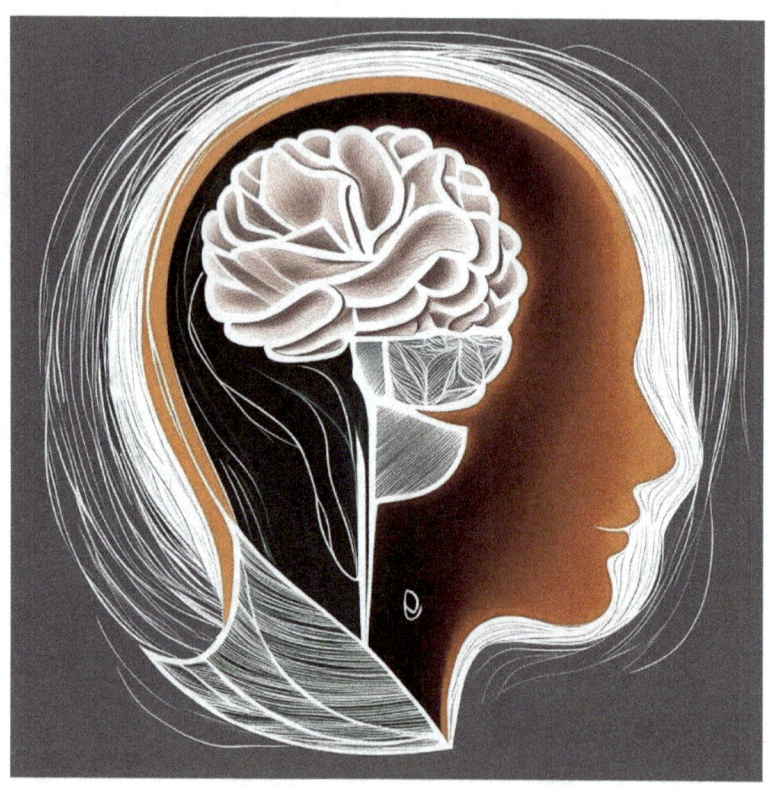

"The mind is everything. What you think you become."
— Buddha

The Importance of Mindset in Parenting

The mindset we adopt as parents deeply influences not only our own experiences but also the development of our children. When we approach parenting with a growth mindset, we open the door to resilience, adaptability, and emotional intelligence. This perspective allows us to view challenges not as obstacles but as invaluable opportunities for both our children and us to learn and grow. By embracing the belief that we can improve and evolve, we set a powerful example for our children, teaching them that setbacks can serve as fuel as we blaze our unique path to success.

Intentional parenting is rooted in self-awareness and the ability to reflect on our thoughts and behaviors. When we cultivate a positive mindset, we become more attuned to our reactions and choices in various situations. This awareness empowers us to respond thoughtfully rather than react impulsively, fostering a nurturing environment where our children feel safe to express themselves. By modeling this thoughtful approach, we encourage our children to develop their own reflective practices, equipping them with the tools they need to navigate life's challenges with confidence and grace.

A growth mindset also encourages us to embrace failure as part of the learning process. In parenting, this mindset shift can be transformative. Instead of fearing mistakes, we can view them as opportunities to teach our children about resilience, problem-solving, and perseverance. When we openly share our own struggles and the lessons learned from them, we normalize the experience of making mistakes. This not only strengthens our relationship with our children but also instills in them the belief that they can overcome difficulties, fostering an unshakeable sense of self-efficacy.

In our next activity, you will explore the concepts of fixed and growth mindsets and examine how these perspectives influence not only your personal development but also the dynamics within your family.

Remember that a fixed mindset tends to view abilities and intelligence as static, leading to a reluctance to embrace challenges and learn from failure. In contrast, a growth mindset promotes the belief that skills and intelligence can be developed through effort and perseverance. As you reflect on your own mindset, consider how it affects your approach to parenting, your responses to your children's challenges, and the overall atmosphere of learning in your home. This activity will encourage you to evaluate your mindset and its implications for fostering resilience, curiosity, and a love of learning in your family, ultimately guiding you toward more supportive and empowering interactions with your children.

Moreover, the importance of mindset extends beyond our individual parenting strategies; it shapes the family dynamic as a whole. A family that collectively adopts a growth mindset fosters an atmosphere of collaboration and support. When challenges arise, family members are more likely to come together, brainstorm solutions, and learn from each other. This collaborative spirit not only strengthens familial bonds but also nurtures a culture of continuous learning and improvement that can last a lifetime, creating an environment where everyone feels empowered to grow.

Embracing a positive mindset in parenting paves the way for nurturing well-rounded individuals who are equipped to face the world. By prioritizing our own mindset and encouraging our children to do the same, we create a legacy of resilience, adaptability, and emotional intelligence. As we navigate the complexities of motherhood, let us remember that our mindset is the lens through which we view our parenting journey. By transforming challenges into growth opportunities, we not only enrich our own lives but also empower the next generation to rise and thrive.

MINDSET SHIFT

Self-Reflection:
Consider whether your current parenting mindset leans more towards growth or is fixed. How does this mindset influence your parenting style and your interactions with your children? What steps can you take to foster a growth mindset for both yourself and your children?

Strategies to Cultivate Resilience

Resilience is not merely a trait; it is a skill that can be cultivated and nurtured. For parents and professionals alike, developing resilience is crucial in navigating the inevitable challenges of life. One effective strategy to build resilience is to foster a growth mindset. As we've discussed, this involves embracing challenges as opportunities for growth rather than obstacles to be avoided. When parents model a growth mindset for their children, they instill a belief that effort and perseverance can lead to improvement. Encouraging open discussions about failures and successes helps normalize the ups and downs of life, reinforcing the idea that setbacks can positively impact our path to success.

Another powerful strategy is the practice of mindfulness. Mindfulness encourages individuals to stay present and engaged in the moment, helping to alleviate stress and anxiety. For parents, incorporating mindfulness into daily routines can create a calm and supportive environment for everyone. Simple practices, such as deep breathing exercises or mindful walking, can be integrated into family activities, allowing everyone to reconnect with their emotions and thoughts. This focus on the present can enhance emotional regulation, enabling both parents and children to respond to challenges with clarity and composure.

Building a strong support network is also essential in cultivating resilience. Parents often face unique pressures and challenges, and having a community of understanding individuals can provide the necessary encouragement and perspective. Whether through friendships, family connections, support groups, or professional networks, creating a circle of support fosters a sense of belonging and shared experience. Parents can also encourage their children to build relationships with peers, teaching them the value of collaboration and mutual support. This network becomes a vital resource during tough times, reminding individuals that they are not alone in their struggles.

Emphasizing the importance of self-care cannot be overstated in the journey toward resilience. Parents often prioritize their children's needs above their own, but neglecting self-care can lead to burnout and diminished capacity to support others. By modeling self-care practices, such as regular exercise, creative pursuits, or simply taking time for rest, parents demonstrate to their children that taking care of oneself is essential for overall well-being. This balance enables parents to be more present and engaged, fostering a nurturing environment where resilience can thrive.

Moreover, instilling a sense of purpose and meaning can significantly enhance resilience. Encouraging children to explore their passions, set goals, and contribute to their communities fosters a sense of agency and direction. Parents can guide their children in identifying their values and exploring ways to align their actions with those values. This sense of purpose acts as a powerful anchor during challenging times, reminding everyone involved that difficulties could lead to meaningful growth and transformation.

Other effective coping strategies that can help strengthen your resilience include,

❖ *Setting Realistic Expectations:* Embrace the idea that perfection is not the goal; set achievable goals for both yourself and your children to reduce stress and create a more positive environment.

❖ *Reflecting on Your Achievements:* Take time to acknowledge your successes, both big and small, to foster a sense of accomplishment and boost your confidence.

In the upcoming activity, you will have the opportunity to develop two personalized coping strategies that resonate with you and your unique circumstances. Following this, you'll respond to the open prompt, "I am strong because ___." This reflection will encourage you to recognize your inner strength and resilience, reinforcing the qualities that empower you as a mother. Let's take this time to delve deeper into your personal coping mechanisms and celebrate your strength!

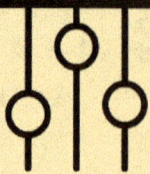

RESILIENCE TOOLKIT

Generate two strategies that can support you in building greater resilience. Consider techniques, practices, or activities that resonate with you and can be integrated into your daily routine.

STRATEGY 1

STRATEGY 2

Respond to the prompt, allowing yourself grace:

"I am strong because _____."

Family Engagement Opportunity

Mindset Board

As a family, brainstorm a list of common fixed mindset beliefs (e.g., "I'm not good at math," "I'm not creative"). Write each fixed mindset belief on a sticky note and place it on a board. For each fixed mindset belief, brainstorm ways to challenge it and replace it with a growth mindset belief (e.g., "I can learn math with practice and effort," "I can be creative if I'm willing to try new things"). Write the growth mindset beliefs on sticky notes and place them next to the corresponding fixed mindset beliefs.

Chapter 7:
Nurturing Self-Compassion

"You, yourself, as much as anybody in the entire universe,
deserve your love and affection."

— Buddha

The Role of Self-Compassion in Motherhood

In the journey of motherhood, self-compassion often takes a backseat to the demands of raising children and managing daily responsibilities. Many times, we find ourselves caught in a cycle of self-criticism, constantly measuring our worth against external standards and the expectations placed upon us. However, recognizing the importance of self-compassion can transform this narrative. It is essential to acknowledge that we are doing our best, navigating the intricacies of challenges and systems, and that it's okay to celebrate our efforts, even if no one else does. Taking a moment to pat yourself on the back can be a powerful reminder of your resilience and strength.

Embracing self-compassion allows us to shift our perspective from one of judgment to one of understanding. When you approach yourself with kindness, you cultivate an inner environment that encourages growth and acceptance. This gentle approach enables you to recognize your accomplishments, no matter how small they may seem. For instance, if you managed to prepare a healthy meal despite a chaotic day, or successfully navigated a tough conversation with your child, these moments deserve recognition. I personally take great pride in my ability to learn new hair styling techniques on the fly, for example, often based on my children's wishes or the latest trends circulating around us. While the end result may not always be picture-perfect, it typically turns out to be acceptable—and more importantly, it reflects my willingness to adapt and respond to my children's desires. This practice of acknowledging both the small victories and the larger accomplishments fuels my confidence as a mother. I invite you to take a moment to reflect on your own journey in the next activity. Whether you recognize it or not, you've been shining brightly throughout this entire journey.

Your "wow" could've been mastering a new recipe, engaging in meaningful conversations, or simply making it through a hectic day with a smile, jotting these down will help you cultivate a deeper sense of appreciation for yourself and the unique ways you contribute to your family's life. Acknowledging your efforts fosters a sense of pride and reinforces your capacity as a mother. It is a practice that builds confidence and nurtures your well-being.

At several distinct instances, answer the following prompt:

TODAY, I AM PROUD OF MYSELF FOR _____.

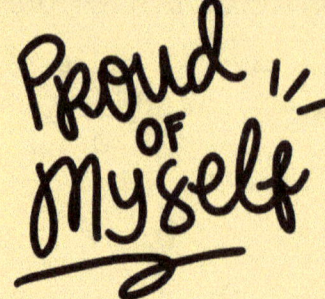

"The greatest victory is not fighting thousands of battles and conquering a thousand foes, but overcoming yourself." - Gautama Buddha

Moreover, remaining humble while embracing your remarkable qualities and actions is a delicate balance. I recently joined a worldwide movement which highlights just that. Humility doesn't require you to diminish your achievements; rather, it invites you to honor your unique journey. Each of our story is filled with moments of bravery, sacrifice, and love. By recognizing your own remarkable aspects—such as your ability to adapt, your creativity in problem-solving, or your unwavering support—you create a space for gratitude and self-acceptance. This humility nurtures connection, not only with yourself but also with others, as it encourages a shared understanding of the challenges and victories inherent in motherhood.

In our next activity, we will take a moment to celebrate your uniqueness by identifying one strength, one ability, and one accomplishment that exemplify why you are truly remarkable. This reflective exercise encourages you to recognize the qualities that set you apart and contribute to your journey as a mother and individual. By highlighting these aspects, you can foster a greater appreciation for yourself and the positive impact you have on those around you. Take a moment to shine a light on what makes you exceptional!

The act of self-compassion serves as a model for our children. By demonstrating kindness towards ourselves, we teach them the importance of self-love and acceptance. This creates a ripple effect, fostering a generation that values emotional well-being and resilience. In cultivating self-compassion, we not only empower ourselves but also lay the foundation for our children to embrace their own remarkable qualities.

By practicing self-compassion, we honor our path and acknowledge the amazing aspects of who we are beyond our role as a mother. Children learn by observing their parents, and when they see us practicing self-compassion, they are more likely to adopt those values themselves. It's essential to remember that while external validation is fleeting, the relationship we nurture with ourselves is enduring. Celebrate your journey, recognize your worth, and embrace the notion that you are indeed remarkable, amazing, generous, and valuable. In doing so, you not only uplift your own spirit but also inspire those around you to appreciate their own unique qualities and experiences.

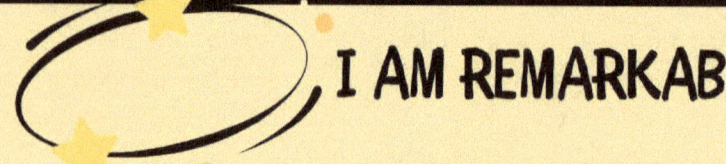

I AM REMARKABLE!

List at least 1 of your strengths, abilities and accomplishments.

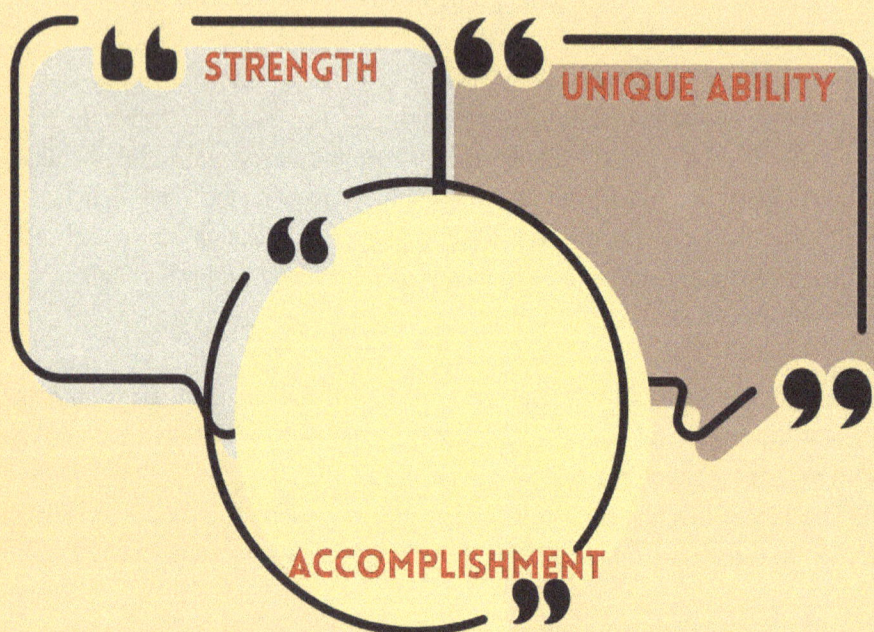

STRENGTH

UNIQUE ABILITY

ACCOMPLISHMENT

Craft a statement that can serve as a constant reminder of why you are remarkable in your own right.

PERSONAL STATEMENT

Practical Exercises for Self-Compassion

In the journey of motherhood, the delicate balance between nurturing our children and honoring our own needs can often feel like a tightrope walk. Self-compassion can be particularly valuable where the pressures and challenges can sometimes lead to self-criticism and doubt. Practical exercises in self-compassion become crucial as we navigate the complexities of parenting. One essential exercise we have mentioned earlier in this book is to establish clear boundaries that honor both your individual needs and those of your children. Yet, below are several practical exercises I find particularly useful in developing a more nurturing relationship with yourself.

Exercise 1. A Self-Compassion Break: This exercise involves taking a few moments to pause and acknowledge your feelings when you experience difficulty or disappointment. Begin by recognizing the emotions you are facing—whether it's frustration, sadness, or overwhelm. Next, remind yourself that it's okay to feel this way; you are not alone in your struggles. Finally, offer yourself words of comfort, similar to what you would say to a friend in a similar situation. For example, you might say, "It's understandable to feel overwhelmed; I'm doing the best I can." This practice helps to normalize your experiences and fosters a sense of connection with yourself.

Exercise 2. Compassionate Letter Writing: Set aside some time to write a letter to yourself from the perspective of a compassionate friend. In this letter, acknowledge your challenges and express understanding and support. Highlight your strengths and remind yourself of the positive qualities you possess. This exercise allows you to step outside of your critical inner dialogue and cultivate a more loving and supportive narrative about yourself. When you read the letter, take a moment to absorb the compassion and warmth it conveys, allowing it to resonate within you.

Exercise 3. Mindful Self-Compassion Meditation: Engaging in mindfulness meditation is a powerful way to enhance self-compassion. Find a quiet space where you can sit comfortably and focus on your breath. As thoughts arise, acknowledge them without judgment and gently guide your attention back to your breath. After a few minutes, introduce loving-kindness phrases, such as "May I be happy, may I be healthy, may I be safe, may I live with ease." This practice helps to create a sense of inner peace and reinforces the importance of caring for yourself, particularly during challenging times.

By incorporating these and similar exercises into your daily or weekly routine, you can nurture a greater sense of self-compassion. As you learn to treat yourself with more kindness and understanding, you will find that your relationship with yourself improves, ultimately leading to a more positive and resilient approach to both motherhood and life. Remember, self-compassion is not a destination but a practice—one that requires patience and dedication. Embrace this journey as an opportunity to grow and flourish in your unique role as a mother and individual.

Similarly, I have included the next activity to help you reflect on your daily schedule and identify moments dedicated solely to yourself—whether it's savoring a quiet cup of coffee, taking a refreshing walk, scrolling self-help content online, or immersing yourself in a few pages of a good book. These small, intentional breaks are essential for recharging your mind and spirit, yet they can often be overlooked in the hustle and bustle of daily life. By intentionally carving out time for yourself, you create opportunities to reconnect with your interests and passions, fostering a sense of balance and well-being. In this activity, you will think about your daily routine and pinpoint those precious moments that allow for self-care and reflection. As you engage in this exercise, consider not only how these moments benefit you but also how they can enhance your ability to be present and engaged with your family. Prioritizing self-care isn't just a luxury—it's a vital component of effective parenting, enabling you to show up as your best self for both yourself and your loved ones. Take this time to honor the importance of self-dedication and discover how even the smallest moments can have a significant impact on your overall well-being.

ME TIME

USE THIS WEEK SNAPSHOT TO THINK ABOUT THE UPCOMING DAYS AND IDENTIFY OPPORTUNITIES FOR SELF-CARE ACTIVITIES.

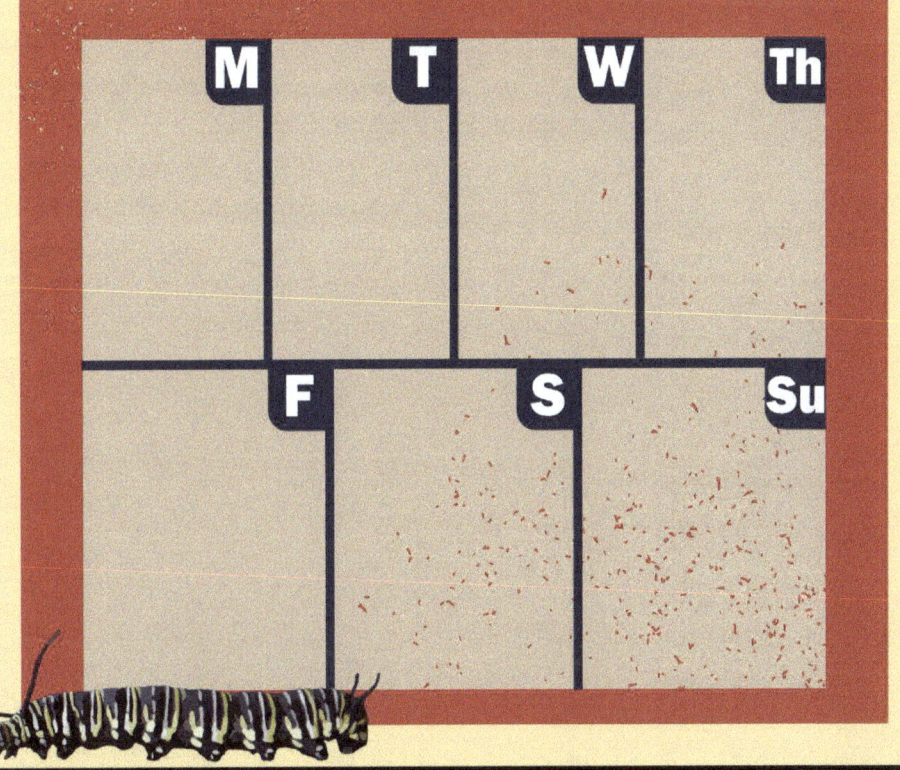

M	T	W	Th

F	S	Su

A Plan for Self-Care

The last activity likely highlighted how the task of identifying and implementing self-care practices is easier said than done. We've established that it is crucial to remind yourself that you cannot pour from an empty cup. We've embraced the idea that it is okay to prioritize your well-being. We've stressed the need to carve out moments to implement activities. Now what? How do we foster an ability to implement self-care? Curating a self-care toolkit will empower you to prioritize activities that recharge and rejuvenate you, making self-care planning more effective.

In the following pages, you'll find several self-care activities designed to inspire and help you brainstorm ways to nurture your well-being. These activities are organized into seven categories, making it easier for you to explore diverse options that resonate with your interests and lifestyle. Each activity includes fields for you to indicate whether you can do it now, later, or if it doesn't appeal to you at all (or "never"). This flexible approach encourages you to prioritize self-care in a way that feels authentic to you, without the pressure of rigid expectations. Remember, these categories are not exhaustive; feel free to adapt or expand upon the ideas to align with your unique preferences and circumstances. I also include a free space with each list to jot down any essential tasks that need to be addressed before you can move forward with your plans. Just like you can't attend a concert without an entry ticket, it's important to acknowledge the necessary steps that pave the way for your goals. Similarly, you can't stream your favorite music without an active subscription. Remember, both the "what" and the "how" are crucial in ensuring your plans come to fruition. The underlying goal is to empower you to find joy and fulfillment in your self-care journey. By nurturing yourself, you cultivate a deeper well of compassion, enabling you to respond to your children's needs with patience and understanding.

When you demonstrate the importance of balancing individual needs with those of others, you create an environment of resilience and empathy. Remember, your journey is not just about meeting the needs of your children; it is also about honoring your own path. By embracing these practical exercises, you transform parenting challenges into opportunities for growth, inspiring your children to cultivate their own self-compassion as they navigate their unique journeys.

SELF-CARE IDEAS: MIND & BODY

Now	Later	Never	
			Mindful Meditation: Train your mind to focus and bring about a state of calm and heightened awareness.
			Deep Breathing Exercises: Practice techniques like diaphragmatic breathing, box breathing, and pursed lip breathing.
			Yoga or Pilates: Improve flexibility, strength, and balance.
			Regular Exercise: Find an activity you enjoy, like walking, running, dancing.
			Mind Mapping: Visualize your ideas and goals.
			Healthy Eating: Focus on whole foods, fruits, vegetables, and lean protein.
			Hydration: Drink plenty of water throughout the day.
			Quality Sleep: Aim for 7-9 hours of uninterrupted sleep.
			Massage: Treat yourself to a professional massage or give yourself a self-massage.
			Aromatherapy: Use essential oils to promote relaxation and reduce stress.
			Healthy Cooking Classes: Learn to prepare nutritious and delicious meals.
			Mindful Eating: Pay attention to your food and savor each bite.
			Mindfulness Walks: Pay attention to your senses while walking in nature.

NOTES TO MAKE IT HAPPEN:

SELF-CARE IDEAS:
PERSONAL GROWTH

Now	Later	Never	
			Set Goals: Define your goals and create a plan to achieve them.
			TED Talks: Watch inspiring talks to gain new perspectives.
			Online Course: Learn a new skill or enhance your professional development.
			Mentoring a Young Professional: Give back by mentoring someone starting their career.
			Public Speaking Workshop: Improve your communication and presentation skills.
			Financial Planning Consultation: Review your financial goals and create a plan.
			Affirmations: Repeat positive affirmations to boost your self-esteem.
			Practice Self-Compassion: Be kind and forgiving to yourself.
			Learn to Say "No": Set boundaries and prioritize your own needs.
			Forgive Yourself: Let go of past mistakes and move forward.
			Read a Book: Lose yourself in a good book to learn something new or forget about your worries.
			Celebrate Your Accomplishments: Acknowledge and appreciate your successes.
			Listen to a Podcast: Learn something new or be entertained.
			Learn a New Language: Challenge your mind and expand your horizons.

NOTES TO MAKE IT HAPPEN:

SELF-CARE IDEAS:
SOCIAL CONNECTION

Now	Later	Never	
			Have a Girls' Night In: Spend quality time with friends, chat, and laugh.
			Join a Book Club: Discuss books with other book lovers.
			Attend a Workshop or Class: Learn a new skill or connect with others who share your interests.
			Volunteer at a Local Non-Profit: Give back to the community, build relationships, and extend your sense of purpose.
			Join a Social Club: Connect with people who share your hobbies and interests.
			Spend Time with Loved Ones: Connect with friends and family.
			Play Board Games: Have fun and connect with others.
			Attend Local Events: Explore local culture, meet new people, and support local businesses.
			Host a Gathering: Creates a welcoming space for others, strengthens existing relationships, and builds new connections.
			Join a Professional Women's Group: Enjoy networking, mentorship, support, and shared experiences.
			Offer Your Professional Skills: Offer pro bono consulting services to showcase your expertise and build connections.
			Engage in Online Communities: Connect with people who share similar interests and build a virtual support network.
			Attend Community Board Meetings: Stay informed about local issues, contribute to community decisions, and connect with local leaders.

NOTES TO MAKE IT HAPPEN:

SELF-CARE IDEAS:
IN-HOME CARE

Now	Later	Never	
			Clean and Organize: Declutter your living space and create a sense of order.
			Cook a Nourishing Meal: Enjoy the process of cooking and savor the flavors and aromas of a home-cooked meal.
			Plant Flowers or Herbs: Connect with nature by gardening and incorporate plants into your home decor.
			Declutter and Organize: Create a sense of calm and order in your living space.
			Decorate: Add personal touches throughout your home.
			Home Spa Treatments: Indulge in at-home spa treatments like a warm bath, a face mask, or a massage
			Cozy Up: Wear your favorite pajamas, grab a blanket, and relax.
			Aromatherapy: Use essential oils to enhance your mood and relaxation.
			Relaxation Zone: Designate a specific area in your home to rest and rejuvenate.
			Warm Atmosphere: Use soft lighting, incense, candles, or essential oil diffusers to create a cozy and inviting ambiance in your home.
			Digital Detox: Designate specific times of day or areas in your home as "tech-free zones."
			Mindful Chores: Practice mindfulness while performing household chores. Focus on the present moment and savor the process of cleaning, cooking, or gardening.

NOTES TO MAKE IT HAPPEN:

SELF-CARE IDEAS: STRESS RELIEF

Now	Later	Never	
			Take a Warm Bath: Relax in a warm bath with Epsom salts and essential oils.
			Acupuncture: Experience the calming effects of acupuncture.
			Travel Solo: Explore a new destination and enjoy some alone time.
			Listen to Audiobooks: Learn while commuting or during downtime.
			Declutter Your Workspace: Create a more organized and productive work environment.
			Listen to Relaxing Noise: Calm your mind with soothing sounds.
			Practice Progressive Muscle Relaxation: Tense and release different muscle groups.
			Spend Time with Pets: Cuddle with your furry friend or play with them.
			Coloring Books: Engage your creativity with adult coloring books.
			Puzzles: Challenge your mind with a jigsaw puzzle, Suduko, or a crossword puzzle.
			Simply Be: Take some time for yourself to do absolutely nothing.
			Watch a Movie: Enjoy a relaxing and entertaining movie.
			Take a Nap: Rest and recharge your batteries.
			Journaling: Reflect on your thoughts, feelings, and experiences.

NOTES TO MAKE IT HAPPEN:

SELF-CARE IDEAS:
SPIRIT & SOUL

Now	Later	Never	
			Spend Time in Nature: Connect with the natural world and find tranquility. Go for a hike, visit a park, or simply enjoy the outdoors.
			Listen to Music: Create a playlist that uplifts and inspires you.
			Read a Book: Get lost in a good book and escape reality for a while.
			Watch a Movie: Enjoy a feel-good movie or a classic.
			Dance: Let loose and move your body to the rhythm of the music.
			Laugh Out Loud: Watch funny videos, read jokes, or spend time with humorous people.
			Declutter: Clear the clutter from your physical and mental space.
			Declutter Your Wardrobe: Donate or sell clothes you no longer wear.
			Declutter Your Digital Life: Delete unused apps and unsubscribe from unwanted emails.
			Connect with Your Spirituality: Explore your spiritual beliefs and practices.
			Meditation: Practice mindfulness and cultivate inner peace.
			Yoga: Connect with your body and mind through yoga.
			Listen to Relaxing Sounds: Calm your mind with soothing sounds.
			Practice Gratitude: Focus on the positive aspects of your life.

NOTES TO MAKE IT HAPPEN:

SELF-CARE IDEAS: PAMPER & INDULGE

Now	Later	Never	
			Indulge in a Massage: Treat yourself to a professional massage or give yourself a self-massage.
			Enjoy a Spa Day: Indulge in a luxurious spa experience.
			Indulge in a Sweet Treat: Have a piece of cake, eat some ice cream, or enjoy a dessert.
			Buy Yourself Flowers: Brighten up your space with a beautiful bouquet.
			Buy a New Outfit: Treat yourself to something new and stylish.
			Go Window Shopping: Enjoy browsing through stores and window displays.
			Spa Day at Home: Face mask, hair mask, bath bombs, the works!
			Manicure/Pedicure: Treat yourself to a professional treatment or do it yourself.
			Hair Treatments: Deep condition, try a new hairstyle, or get a professional trim.
			Skincare Routine: Develop a consistent skincare routine that suits your needs.
			Makeup-Free Days: Embrace your natural beauty and go makeup-free.
			Bubble Bath: Relax in a warm bath with soothing scents and music.

NOTES TO MAKE IT HAPPEN:

Family Engagement Opportunity

One-on-One

Schedule a series of one-on-one discussions with each of your children to explore their individual needs, interests, and goals. After these conversations, hold a family meeting to openly share insights and any changes that may arise. This will help identify opportunities for continuous improvement in your shared family experiences.

Chapter 8:
Effective Communication with Your Children

"The single biggest problem in communication
is the illusion that it has taken place."
— George Bernard Shaw

Listening to Understand

Listening to understand is an essential skill for parents and professionals alike, serving as a bridge between communication and connection. In an age where distractions abound, the art of listening often takes a backseat to the noise of daily life. However, when we consciously choose to listen with the intent to understand, we open doors to deeper relationships and richer experiences. This practice invites us to step into the shoes of others, fostering empathy and compassion, which are vital in both parenting and professional environments.

To listen with intention means to set aside our own thoughts, judgments, and responses. It requires us to be fully present in the moment, creating a safe space for our children or colleagues to express themselves. This kind of listening goes beyond hearing words; it involves tuning into emotions, body language, and the unspoken nuances of a conversation. When we make the effort to grasp the underlying messages, we validate the feelings of others and encourage open, honest dialogue. This validation can be transformative, allowing individuals to feel seen and valued.

In the realm of motherhood, listening to understand can significantly impact our relationships with our children. Young minds often struggle to articulate their feelings, and by listening attentively, we can decode their needs and offer support. This practice nurtures trust and strengthens our bond, empowering our children to express themselves freely. As parents, we can model effective communication, teaching our children the importance of listening and understanding in their interactions with peers and adults alike. The lessons learned at home will echo into their future relationships, fostering a generation that values connection.

As a professional, you can also harness the power of listening to enhance their workplace dynamics. In team settings, understanding one another's perspectives leads to collaboration and innovation. Leaders who listen actively cultivate an environment where team members feel safe to share ideas and concerns. This open communication fuels creativity and problem-solving, essential components in today's fast-paced world. When we prioritize listening, we not only improve our professional relationships but also contribute to a culture of respect and inclusivity.

Ultimately, listening to understand is an intentional practice that enriches our lives and the lives of those around us. It challenges us to step away from our own narratives and embrace the stories of others. In motherhood, it nurtures our children's growth, helping them develop their voice. In professional settings, it enhances collaboration and fosters a sense of belonging. By committing to this practice, we embark on a journey of growth, transforming challenges into opportunities for deeper connections and understanding. Embrace this powerful tool and watch as your relationships flourish.

Self-Awareness in Communication

Self-awareness in communication is a vital skill that allows us to recognize how our words, tone, and body language affect our interactions with others, particularly our children. Being mindful of our communication style helps us to identify our strengths and areas for improvement, fostering more meaningful connections. This awareness enables us to reflect on how our emotions and experiences influence the way we express ourselves and respond to our children's needs. As we prepare to conduct a SWOT analysis, we will delve deeper into this self-awareness by assessing our communication practices.

By examining our strengths, weaknesses, opportunities, and threats, we can gain valuable insights into how to enhance our interactions, ultimately leading to healthier and more effective communication within our families. This analysis will serve as a foundation for developing strategies that bolster our relationships and support our children's emotional growth.

By identifying your strengths, you can pinpoint what works well in your interactions, such as your ability to listen empathetically or create a safe space for open dialogue, which fosters connection and understanding. Conversely, exploring your weaknesses will help you recognize areas where improvement is needed, such as moments of frustration or miscommunication that may hinder effective interaction.

Then, you will consider the opportunities available for enhancing your communication. This could include incorporating new technique or finding creative ways to engage in conversations during everyday activities. I sometimes find it challenging to brainstorm opportunities because we often don't know what we don't know. To help you get started, here are a few techniques you can use to spark your creativity and uncover new possibilities that may work for you and your family:

❖ *Active Listening Practices:* Set aside dedicated time to listen to your children without distractions, showing them that their thoughts and feelings are valued.

❖ *Open-Ended Questions:* Encourage deeper conversations by asking open-ended questions that require more than a yes or no answer, prompting your children to share their thoughts and feelings.

❖ *Family Meetings:* Establish regular family meetings where everyone can express their opinions, discuss plans, and address any concerns in a supportive environment.

❖ Storytelling Time: Share stories from your own life or ask your children to share theirs, fostering a two-way dialogue that enhances understanding and connection.

❖ *Use of Visual Aids:* Incorporate visual aids or tools, such as charts or drawings, to help explain complex topics or emotions, making it easier for children to grasp concepts.

❖ *Role-Playing:* Engage in role-playing scenarios to practice handling difficult conversations, helping children develop their communication skills in a safe setting.

❖ *Mindfulness Practices:* Introduce mindfulness exercises, such as breathing techniques or meditation, to help calm emotions and promote clearer communication during challenging discussions.

❖ *Setting Aside One-on-One Time:* Dedicate special time to each child individually to strengthen your bond and encourage them to express themselves more freely.

❖ *Encouraging Expression Through Art:* Allow children to express their feelings through drawing, writing, or other creative outlets, and then discuss their creations together.

❖ *Modeling Healthy Communication:* Demonstrate effective communication skills, such as using "I" statements and respectful language, to set a positive example for your children to follow.

Finally, assessing potential threats—such as external distractions, time constraints, or emotional stressors—will enable you to develop strategies to minimize their impact on your communication with your children.

By taking a comprehensive look at these four aspects (strengths, weaknesses, opportunities, and threats), this reflective exercise aims to deepen your awareness of how you communicate, ultimately leading to more meaningful and effective interactions that support your children's emotional growth and foster a nurturing family environment. Embracing this analysis empowers you not only to improve your communication skills but also to strengthen your overall relationship with your children.

SWOT

Consider your communication style with your children and jot down at least one strength, one weakness, one opportunity for improvement, and one potential threat. Afterward, reflect on your observations and insights regarding how these elements impact your interactions and relationship with your children.

STRENGTH

WEAKNESS

OPPORTUNITY

THREAT

REFLECTIONS

Speaking with Intention

Speaking with intention is a powerful practice that shapes our relationships and influences the environment we create for our children. Each word we choose carries weight, not just in meaning but in the energy it conveys. When we speak with intention, we are mindful of our language, recognizing that our words can uplift, empower, and inspire those around us. As parents and professionals, embracing this practice can transform our interactions, fostering an atmosphere of growth and understanding.

In the realm of motherhood and parenting, our words set the tone for our children's experiences. When we communicate with clarity and purpose, we model the importance of thoughtful expression. Children absorb our language and the emotions behind it, learning to navigate their own feelings and relationships. By speaking with intention, we teach them to articulate their thoughts and emotions effectively, paving the way for open dialogue and connection. This practice can be a catalyst for emotional intelligence, allowing our children to flourish in their understanding of themselves and others.

Moreover, intentional speaking extends beyond our immediate family. In professional settings, the way we communicate can significantly impact our influence and leadership. When we approach conversations with a clear intention, we engage others more deeply, fostering collaboration and trust. This intentionality encourages us to listen actively, respond thoughtfully, and offer support where it is needed. In turn, this cultivates a sense of community and belonging, essential elements for both personal and professional growth.

Embracing the habit of speaking with intention also invites us to reflect on our own beliefs and values. As we become more aware of the messages we send, we can align our words with our true intentions. This alignment empowers us to communicate authentically, ensuring that our interactions resonate with sincerity and purpose. By doing so, we not only inspire those around us but also reinforce our commitment to personal growth and development, modeling the very principles we wish to instill in our children.

One effective way to speak with intention is through affirmations. In our next activity, we will focus on creating positive affirmations for both ourselves and our children as a powerful way to enhance communication and foster a supportive environment. Positive affirmations are simple yet impactful statements that reinforce our self-worth and encourage a growth mindset.

By crafting affirmations tailored to our unique experiences and challenges, we can empower ourselves to communicate with confidence and compassion. Additionally, creating affirmations for our children can help them build their self-esteem and encourage open expression of thoughts and feelings. As we engage in this activity, you will explore the importance of positive language and its transformative effect on our interactions. Let's leverage this opportunity to cultivate uplifting messages that not only strengthen our own communication skills but also nurture a positive atmosphere for our children to thrive.

In the end, speaking with intention is an act of respect—both for ourselves and for those we engage with. It requires us to pause, consider, and choose our words wisely, recognizing the profound impact they hold. By adopting this practice in our daily lives, we can transform challenges into opportunities for growth, fostering a nurturing environment that encourages our children to thrive. With each intentional word, we contribute to a legacy of empowerment and understanding, shaping not only our lives but the lives of those we cherish.

Think of ways to express words of affirmation to your children and yourself regularly, such as complimenting their efforts, expressing gratitude for their qualities, or offering support and encouragement. Two example affirmations are provided to help you get started. Aim to create at least one unique affirmation for each child, reflecting their individual strengths. Once you've crafted your affirmations, share them promptly to foster a culture of positivity and encouragement in your home.

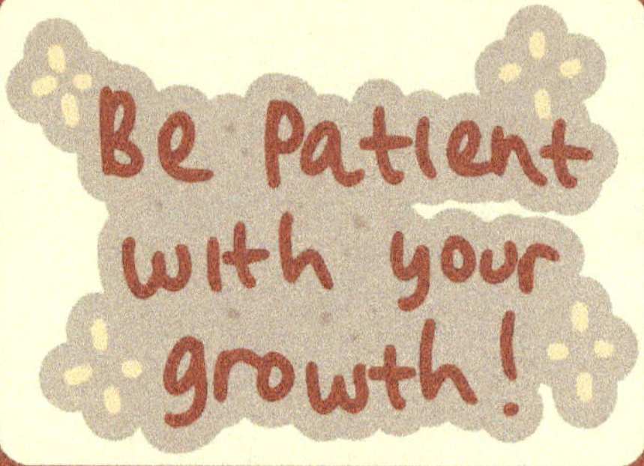

L♥VE yourself

Be Patient with your growth!

Family Engagement Opportunity

Family Assembly

Schedule regular family meetings to discuss important topics, share thoughts and feelings, and collaboratively make decisions. These gatherings provide a supportive space for open communication and strengthen family bonds.

Family Storytime

Encourage family members to read aloud to each other, even if you have little ones that use the pictures to narrate the stories. At any point in the story, the person reading can say "SHIFT" (or some other word your family agrees upon) which requires the next reader to jump in and choose to make up the next part of the story or continue reading. This will provide an opportunity to model effective communication and storytelling in a fun, and engaging way.

Chapter 9:
Creating a Supportive Community

"None of us can win if some of us lose, especially when those who are losing are the most vulnerable."

—Madeleine Albright

An Inherent and Broad Skillset

In the journey of intentional motherhood, recognizing and honing the inherent skills we possess can be transformative. We return to this topic in this chapter to explore it further. The archetype of the "ultimately skilled woman" embodies a diverse array of talents that seamlessly intertwine to create a harmonious family life. From party planning to teaming to household chores, this multifaceted individual exemplifies how embracing various roles not only enhances our capabilities but also enriches our relationships with our children, partners and co-workers. By acknowledging these skills, we can foster an environment that nurtures growth and creativity, empowering our families to thrive.

For example, one of my favorite things to do is to plan a celebration. Party planning may seem like a simple task, yet it encompasses a wealth of skills that extend beyond mere organization. It involves creativity in theme selection, meticulous attention to detail in execution, and the ability to motivate and engage others. When parents take the initiative to celebrate milestones with thoughtful gatherings, they not only strengthen family bonds but also teach children the value of connection and celebration. Each party becomes an opportunity to inspire joy and cultivate memories, reinforcing the importance of family traditions and the power of shared experiences.

The skills I've honed in party planning and celebrating milestones with my family have seamlessly translated into my professional life, enriching my roles as an outreach sponsor, conference exhibitor, and workshop facilitator. Just as I carefully craft memorable experiences for my children—considering their interests, preferences, and the unique themes—I apply the same creativity and attention to detail in my professional endeavors. Whether I'm setting up an engaging booth at a conference or facilitating a workshop on large language models influences on diversity, equity, and inclusion, I draw on my ability to create an inviting atmosphere that fosters connection and engagement. This involves not only meticulous planning but also the flexibility to adapt to the needs of participants, ensuring that everyone feels included and valued.

Celebrating moments with my children has taught me the importance of creating meaningful experiences, and I bring that same enthusiasm and intentionality to my work, transforming professional gatherings into memorable events that inspire and connect individuals in profound ways. So, whether it's a 3-year-old with a snot-bubble encasing a Lego masterpiece, a 33-year-old contemplating a career change or an 83-year-old wishing to reflect on their time working as a space camp counselor in their prime, I am usually ready and eager to engage.

Similarly, household chores can often feel like an endless cycle, but within them lies a treasure trove of life lessons. Engaging children in laundry, cleaning, and cooking fosters a sense of responsibility and teamwork. It teaches them essential skills that they will carry into adulthood while also promoting a sense of accomplishment. When parents approach these tasks with enthusiasm and creativity, they transform mundane chores into enjoyable family activities. This approach not only lightens the load but also instills a strong work ethic and the understanding that contributing to the household is a shared responsibility.

Then, homework, projects and other activities that promote SMART STEAM exposure present another unique avenue for parents to showcase their versatility. Pardon the specific nod to SMART STEAM as that is my not-so-subtle attempt to mention my programming based on systems engineering and STEM. SMART STEAM is intended to promote systems, management, analysis, reading, and thinking skills in addition to more traditional STEM/STEAM (science, technology, engineering, art, and math) skills. Feel free to check out my children's book on a range of related topics.

Nonetheless, by becoming involved in our children's education, we can motivate and inspire a love for learning and thinking critically. Whether working through everyday challenges or more structured exercises and problems, these moments are invaluable opportunities for intentional motherhood and growth. They allow mothers to share their own experiences, encouraging children to dream big, live inspired and embrace challenges [Yes, that is yet another nod to my daughter's journal, Dream Big & Live Inspired for children!]. This synergy between mother and child not only aids academic success but also builds a foundation of curiosity and resilience that will serve them well throughout their lives.

The art of everything we do for our children and our families further highlights the mother's diverse capabilities. From organizing family trips that create lasting memories to creating beautiful decorations for special occasions, these activities require foresight, creativity, and collaboration. By embracing these roles, we can instill a sense of adventure in our children, encouraging them to explore the world with open minds and hearts. Additionally, completing activities together can spark creativity and innovation, allowing our children to express themselves while learning the importance of persistence and problem-solving. Ultimately, acknowledging and celebrating these inherent skills not only enriches our lives as parents but also sets the stage for our children to grow into well-rounded individuals who are ready to take on the world.

In our next activity, we will revisit the idea of overlap between roles and continue to explore the transferability of skills you have developed as a mother and as a professional. This exercise is designed to help you reflect more deeply on the valuable competencies you've gained in both realms and recognize how they can enhance and inform each other. By examining the skills you utilize in your parenting—such as communication, problem-solving, and emotional intelligence—you can identify how these same abilities are applicable in your professional life, and vice versa. Understanding the interconnectedness of these skills not only reinforces your capabilities as a mother and professional but also empowers you to leverage your experiences in one setting to benefit the other. Go ahead and dive into this reflective process to celebrate the rich plethora of skills you possess and the profound impact they have on your life as a whole.

TRANSFERABLE SKILLS

IDENTIFY 1 PARENTING SKILL THAT HAS BEEN USEFUL AT WORK. THEN, IDENTIFY A PROFESSIONAL SKILL FROM WORK OR SCHOOL THAT HAS TRANSLATED TO YOUR ROLE OF PARENTING.

FROM MOTHERHOOD TO WORK

FROM WORK TO MOTHERHOOD

REFLECT ON THE VALUE OF YOUR TRANSFERABLE SKILLS.

The Value of Connection

In our fast-paced world, the value of connection often takes a backseat to our busy schedules and endless responsibilities. Yet, it is precisely those connections that provide the foundation for growth, resilience, and fulfillment. As mothers and professionals, we must recognize that nurturing relationships—whether with our children, partners, colleagues, or friends—can transform our experiences and pave the way for deeper understanding and compassion. By prioritizing these connections, we invite opportunities for personal development and emotional enrichment into our lives.

Connection begins at home, where the bond between mother and child serves as a vital source of support and encouragement. When we engage with our children on a meaningful level, we not only foster their emotional intelligence but also strengthen our own. Active listening, shared experiences, and open conversations create an environment where both parent and child feel valued and understood. These moments of connection become the building blocks for resilience, helping children navigate their challenges with confidence, while reminding us of the power of love and empathy.

The workplace, too, thrives on connection. Building strong relationships with colleagues can lead to enhanced collaboration, creativity, and productivity. As professionals, we can cultivate a culture that values open communication and mutual respect, ultimately transforming challenges into opportunities for collective growth. When we connect with others, we create a support network that empowers us to overcome obstacles and celebrate achievements together. This sense of belonging not only enriches our professional lives but also reinforces our roles as nurturing figures in our families.

Furthermore, the connections we forge outside of our immediate circles— through community involvement, friendships, and networking—enrich our lives in profound ways. Engaging with others who share our interests and values can inspire us to pursue new passions, challenge our perspectives, and embrace diverse viewpoints. These relationships remind us that we are not alone in our journeys; they provide invaluable support and encouragement as we navigate the complexities of motherhood and professional life.

Reflecting on my own journey, I'm deeply grateful for the meaningful connections that have shaped me. My childhood teachers, now some of my biggest cheerleaders, remind me of their early belief in my potential, even as we reminisce about our shared school days more than 30 years ago. A simple data request sparked a profound mentorship with a once-stranger, now a trusted confidant with whom I share conversations about research, life, motherhood, and personal growth. And even my children's teachers have become cherished friends, offering support in and outside the classroom, with several joining us for family outings, and becoming like extended family. These invaluable relationships have enriched my life, demonstrating the power of community and the importance of nurturing those who uplift and inspire us.

In our next activity, we will take time to identify and explore a deep connection you have developed in your lifetime—whether it be with a family member, friend, mentor, or partner. This reflective exercise invites you to explore the emotions and experiences associated with that connection, examining how it has shaped you and influenced your perspective on relationships. Consider how it felt to be truly connected with someone, the sense of support and understanding that came from that bond, and the ways it may have impacted your personal growth and well-being. By articulating the significance of this connection, you will gain valuable insights into the importance of nurturing relationships in your life, ultimately enhancing your understanding of how these connections contribute to your overall sense of fulfillment and resilience.

Ultimately, the value of connection is immeasurable. It fosters resilience, nurtures personal growth, and cultivates a sense of belonging that is essential for our well-being. As we embrace the challenges of parenting and professional life, let us remain intentional about building and nurturing our connections. By doing so, we create a life rich in support, understanding, and shared experiences, transforming not only our own lives but also the lives of those around us. In this journey of intentional motherhood, let the power of connection guide us toward a brighter, more fulfilling future.

DEEP CONNECTIONS

Self-Reflection:

Reflect on a person with whom you have developed a deep connection in your lifetime. How does it feel to experience that level of connection? In what ways has this bond positively influenced your well-being and personal growth?

Building Your Tribe

In the journey of motherhood, the importance of community cannot be overstated. Building your tribe—comprising your faith-based or spiritual center, neighborhood, family, friends, schools, and more—creates a network of support that enriches both your life and the lives of your children. This is especially true for me as I begin my journey as a newly single, co-parent. Each member of this tribe contributes unique perspectives and resources, helping to navigate the challenges of parenting. By intentionally cultivating these relationships, you create a resilient foundation for your family, one that thrives on shared experiences, encouragement, and collective wisdom.

A church may be a cornerstone of your community, offering not only spiritual guidance but also a nurturing environment for your children. Engaging in church activities allows you to connect with other families who share similar values and goals. These interactions can lead to lifelong friendships, playdates for your children, and opportunities for collaborative projects that benefit your community. By participating in church groups or volunteer activities, you model the importance of service and connection to your children, teaching them to reach out and build relationships that matter.

Your neighborhood is another vital element in building your tribe. It is often the first place where your children form friendships and begin to understand their social world. By fostering relationships with your neighbors, you create a sense of belonging and security for your family. Organizing neighborhood gatherings, such as potlucks or playdates, can break down barriers and encourage open communication. These connections can transform your neighborhood into a supportive environment where everyone looks out for one another, making it easier to navigate the ups and downs of parenting.

Family ties are also an essential part of your tribe. Extended family members often provide invaluable support, sharing their wisdom and experiences. Regular family gatherings offer an opportunity for your children to bond with relatives, fostering a sense of identity and continuity. Encourage your children to connect with grandparents, aunts, uncles, and cousins, creating a rich network of relationships that provide love and guidance throughout their lives. Involving family in your journey can also alleviate stress, allowing you to lean on them in times of need.

Friends play a critical role in your support system as well. Surrounding yourself with like- minded individuals who understand the challenges of motherhood can be incredibly empowering. These friendships provide a safe space for sharing experiences, seeking advice, and celebrating victories, big and small. By intentionally cultivating friendships with other parents, you create a network that encourages personal growth and resilience. Schools, too, can be a source of community, where you can connect with other parents and educators who share your commitment to your children's development. Engaging with the school community not only enhances your child's educational experience but also strengthens your tribe, providing a rich environment for collaboration and support.

In our next activity, you will explore your local area to discover opportunities that align with your interests across four broad categories: people, places, spiritual pursuits, and materialistic things. This exploration invites you to research and identify activities, events, or resources that resonate with you and can enrich your life. Jot down contact information so that you can more easily return to it later.

Once you've identified these resources, take the next step: connect! Explore upcoming events, engage with the community, and learn about the various offerings. Remember, everything isn't for everybody, but I can guarantee that somewhere in this universe, there is something, some optimal resource, ready and awaiting you.

Whether it's connecting with community groups, visiting local landmarks, engaging in spiritual practices, or discovering new hobbies and interests, this activity encourages you to broaden your horizons and find inspiration in your surroundings. Take this time to uncover the possibilities that await you in your community and consider how they can enhance your personal growth and fulfillment.

BETTER TOGETHER

Identify resources in your local community that foster networking, support and connection (e.g. churches, small businesses, schools, community centers). Capture at least one form of contact for the entity.

PEOPLE

_____

PLACES

_____

"No man is an island entire of itself; every man is a piece of the continent, a part of the main." - John Donne

_____

SPIRIT

_____

THINGS

Family Engagement Opportunity

Family Support Network

As a family, brainstorm a list of people who provide support and encouragement to you. This could include family members, friends, teachers, coaches, mentors, or community members. In the center of the poster board, write "Our Family Support Network." Draw lines radiating outward from the center. On each sticky note, write the name of a person in your support network. Place the sticky notes on the lines radiating from the center, creating a visual representation of your network. Discuss the map as a family. Talk about the different types of support each person provides, the qualities you admire in your supporters, and how you can show your appreciation for them.

Chapter 10:
Balancing Professional Life and Motherhood

"The key is not to prioritize what's on your schedule, but to schedule your priorities."

— Stephen Covey

Strategies for [Remote] Work-Life Harmony

Remote work has revolutionized the way we approach our professional lives, especially for parents who juggle multiple responsibilities. For those of us who have spent years working from home, the challenge of maintaining a distinct separation between work and home life can feel overwhelming. The blurred lines can lead to an environment where work tasks creep into family time, and personal moments are overshadowed by professional obligations. However, with intention and awareness, it is possible to cultivate strategies that foster a harmonious balance, allowing both work and home life to coexist in a fulfilling way.

Establishing clear boundaries is one of the most effective strategies for achieving work-life harmony. This may involve setting specific work hours that align with your family's schedule, communicating these hours to both colleagues and family members. When everyone is aware of your availability, it becomes easier to create a space where work is prioritized during designated hours, while family time can be fully embraced afterward. Creating a physical workspace that is separate from common family areas can also reinforce this boundary, signaling to both you and your family when you are 'at work' and when you are 'at home.'

Recently, I decided to try a co-working space outside of my home, and it has proven to be a transformative experience for my work productivity. This change of scenery allows me to create a clearer separation between my home life and professional responsibilities, which has been essential in fostering focus and concentration. Surrounded by like-minded individuals, I find the energy and motivation of the co-working environment invigorating, making it easier to immerse myself in my tasks without the usual distractions that come with working from home. It also serves as self-care, as I am constantly meeting new people, discovering social offerings and learning myself in my new role. This intentional shift not only enhances my productivity but also provides a refreshing balance that helps me transition back into my family life with renewed energy and focus.

Routine is another powerful ally in the quest for work-life harmony. Developing a structured daily schedule can provide a sense of predictability and control amidst the chaos of juggling responsibilities. Integrate family rituals and activities into your daily routine, ensuring that quality time is carved out for your loved ones. Whether it's a morning coffee ritual with your partner, lunch break walks with your child, or an evening family game night, these intentional moments can serve as anchors, grounding you in the present and reminding you of what truly matters.

Embracing flexibility is essential in a work environment, especially for parents. While routines are beneficial, life is often unpredictable, and the ability to adapt is key. Allow yourself grace when things don't go as planned. If a work deadline looms, communicate openly with your family about your needs, and involve them in the process. By making them part of your work life, you can foster understanding and support, creating a collaborative environment that honors both professional and personal commitments.

As we wrap up our exploration of work-life balance, it's essential to remember that finding harmony between our professional and personal lives is an ongoing journey that requires patience and self-compassion. Embracing the ebb and flow of responsibilities while carving out moments for ourselves is crucial for nurturing our well-being. By consciously implementing boundaries, routines, and flexibility, parents can transform the remote work experience into an opportunity for deeper connections with both their work and family life.

As we cultivate work-life harmony, we nurture ourselves and model resilience for our children, instilling the importance of balance and intentionality. To symbolize this holistic approach and cultivate a sense of inner peace, I invite you to engage in the next activity: coloring a mandala. This ancient art form offers a powerful opportunity to relax, reflect, and reconnect with your inner self as you express your thoughts and emotions through color.

.I.S.S.
EEPING IT SIMPLE AND SELF-EXPRESSIVE

ure supplies to color this mandala art, a popular practice for stress
uction, mindfulness, creativity, mood modification, patience and therapy.

ess Reduction: The repetitive
e of coloring engages the mind
nd can help to quiet racing
houghts, lower anxiety, and
promote relaxation.

Mindfulness & Focus: Coloring requires
concentration, which can help to improve
focus and increase mindfulness. It can be
a meditative practice that brings
attention to the present moment.

vity & Self-Expression: While
wing a pattern, there's still
or creativity in color choices
hading techniques. It allows
sense of accomplishment and
personal expression.

Improved Mood & Patience: The act of
creating something intricately beautiful can
boost mood and increase feelings of
satisfaction, patience, and well-being.

Prioritizing Well-Being

As parents, the instinct to prioritize our children's needs above our own can feel overwhelming. Society often glorifies the idea of self-sacrifice, painting a picture of a "good parent" as someone who puts their children at the forefront of every decision. However, this mindset can lead to burnout and resentment, ultimately hindering our ability to nurture our children effectively. Recognizing that our well-being is equally important is a crucial step in fostering a healthy family dynamic. By prioritizing our own needs, we set a powerful example for our children about the value of self-care and the importance of maintaining balance in life.

When we take time for ourselves, we recharge our emotional and physical batteries. This replenishment allows us to show up as our best selves, ready to face the challenges of parenting with patience and grace. Whether it's a quiet moment with a book, a jog in the fresh air, or an evening out om the town, these moments of self-care are not indulgences—they are necessities. By carving out space for our well-being, we cultivate resilience and a positive mindset, equipping ourselves to handle the demands of parenthood with renewed energy and enthusiasm.

Moreover, prioritizing our well-being teaches our children invaluable lessons about self-respect and boundaries. Children absorb the behaviors and beliefs of those around them, and by modeling self-care, we instill in them an understanding of their own needs. They learn that it's okay to take a step back and focus on themselves when life gets overwhelming. This creates a ripple effect, encouraging them to develop healthy habits and emotional intelligence as they grow, ultimately fostering their independence and self-advocacy.

It is essential to acknowledge that there will be times when our needs must take precedence. This doesn't mean we love our children any less; rather, it signifies a commitment to being the best version of ourselves for them. Life presents challenges that can feel all-consuming, and recognizing when we need to prioritize our own well-being is a sign of strength, not weakness. By taking care of ourselves, we equip ourselves to better support our children through their challenges, ensuring that we are present and engaged when it matters most.

This realization may be the most profound lesson of my journey thus far.

Prioritizing my own well-being became a critical lesson learned through a painful journey of decline that unfolded after years of operating at full throttle in both my professional and parenting life. At first glance, the breakdown seemed instantaneous, but in hindsight, logic reveals a series of compounding pressures that led to my unraveling. I lost my best friend, and shortly thereafter, my father passed away while visiting me for the holidays. In the midst of these profound losses, the world was hit by the COVID pandemic and then my husband left. Each of these events felt like a heavy blow, and despite the emotional weight they carried, I pushed through, believing that resilience meant continuing to function without pause. However, what I failed to recognize was that each setback was contributing to a silent deterioration within me.

My physical health manifested the consequences of neglecting my own needs during this tumultuous time. In a moment of haste, I fell down the stairs while rushing to a work meeting, resulting in a head injury, chronic back pain, and a twisted tailbone. Rather than taking this as a sign to slow down, I continued to soldier on. Then came two car accidents that further exacerbated my daily pain, leaving me in a constant state of discomfort. My pre-diabetes returned, my heart valve began leaking, and I experienced unsettling memory loss and cognitive decline. A thyroid dysfunction added yet another layer to my already overwhelming struggles. I was essentially dying in plain sight, grappling with depression and anxiety as I felt trapped in a cycle of doing my best under increasingly dire circumstances. Even in my darkest moments, I found myself making excuses to avoid attending to my own needs, perpetuating the downward spiral.

Eventually, I reached a breaking point where I felt paralyzed—mind, body, and spirit. I vividly remember throwing myself onto the floor from my bed, crawling toward my walking cane, desperate to regain some resemblance of functioning. I remember looking around hoping someone would come save me- a doctor, a psychologist, a social worker- unknowingly, the resolution was entangled within much more than what met the eye. I realized that by pressing forward through my struggles, but without taking the time to take care of myself, I'd contributed to my own decline. It became painfully obvious that my current trajectory was unsustainable.

Despite undergoing numerous treatments, including neurological surgery, partial thyroid removal, radiofrequency ablation, hypnosis, and pain therapy, I was still trying to cram these crucial interventions into the margins of my already overflowing schedule. Here are two examples to give you an idea of the gravity of my situation:

My Doctor: "We need to get you scheduled for surgery as soon as possible."

Me: "OK, well I have my children at home so let's aim for a time when they are with their dad. Do you have a slot in the summer (4 months away). I should be fine till then?"

Me: "OMG, I can't seem to catch my breath. I'm having chest palpitations and pain thrusting through my upper body. It hurts so badly." <crying>

Everyone: "Go to the emergency room NOW."

Me: "It's OK. I'll just lay down for a little while. I don't want them to end up keeping me; I don't have anyone to take my children to school in the morning."

These scenarios might seem extreme, but they're not fiction. These conversations, or versions of them, played out repeatedly over the past few years. I even recall a time my employer insisted I go to the ER. There I sat on a gurney in a hallway for hours, waiting for a doctor to clear me. Yet, despite someone else recognizing the urgency of my situation, I ultimately checked myself out before being seen. In my mind, I had to pick up my children from school. The $1500 bill I later received for the limited services only underscored the disconnect: even facing a clear need for medical attention, I still couldn't prioritize my own well-being.

It's a stark irony: here I was, a woman with a terminal degree in engineering, adept at problem-solving and systems design, yet I couldn't, for the life of me (literally), devise a solution to prioritize my own needs and prevent my own premature demise. I could design complex systems, but I couldn't design a life that sustained me once presented with the abundance of change and discord I was facing.

The most effective steps I took turned out to be outside of my specialists' offices- to more actively seek support, ground myself in faith, and intentionally prioritize my well-being. It is a work in progress but I am committed to this purpose. This shift not only allows me to begin deep healing but also reinforces the truth that self-care is not a luxury but a necessity—one that enables us to be present and effective in all areas of our lives, especially as parents. Through my own journey, I reluctantly learned that it is essential to care for ourselves first in order to truly care for others.

In our next activity, we will take a closer look at the obstacles that hinder you from prioritizing your well-being. This reflective exercise is designed to help you identify and examine the various challenges you face in making self-care a priority in your life. Do you find yourself saying any of these statements or thinking these thoughts? Each of these statements imply the presence of self-imposed hindrances.

Time & Scheduling	Guilt & Obligation
"I just don't have time."	"I feel guilty taking time for myself."
"I'm too busy taking care of everyone."	"My family needs me more than I need me."
"There aren't enough hours in the day."	"It's selfish to prioritize my needs over theirs."
"I'll do it later, when things calm down."	"I should be focusing on my children/partner/house."
"My kids' schedules are so demanding."	"I'm the only one who can do it."
"I can't possibly fit anything else in."	"If I don't do it, it won't get done right."
"Weekends are for catching up on everything I didn't have time for during the week."	
Self-Neglect & Low Self-Worth	**Fear & Anxiety**
"I'm not worth it."	"What if something happens while I'm gone?"
"I don't deserve to be pampered/rested/happy."	"I'm afraid of what people will think."
"My needs aren't important."	"I'm worried about falling behind."
"I'm used to putting myself last."	"I don't want to burden anyone."
"It's too much effort."	"I'm afraid of what I'll discover about myself if I slow down."
"I'll just feel more stressed trying to..."	
"I don't even know what I like anymore."	

Social & Cultural Pressures	Lack of Support
"Mothers are supposed to be selfless."	"I don't have anyone to help me."
"I should be able to handle everything."	"My partner/family doesn't support me
"It's just part of being a mom."	taking time for myself."
"Everyone else seems to manage it all."	"I can't afford childcare."
"I don't want to appear weak or needy."	

By thoughtfully considering these obstacles, you can gain a deeper understanding of whether they are genuine external challenges or self-inflicted barriers that stem from limiting beliefs or negative self-talk, like many of my own.

As you engage in this activity, take the time to write down the specific factors that seem to impede your ability to prioritize your well-being. This might include time constraints, responsibilities, or societal expectations. Once you have outlined these obstacles, reflect on each one to determine its legitimacy. Ask yourself whether these challenges are truly insurmountable or if they are influenced by your perceptions or fears. This process of inquiry can reveal patterns in your thinking and behavior that may be holding you back from fully embracing self-care.

Essentially, this activity is about empowerment and awareness. By distinguishing between real challenges and self-imposed limitations, you can begin to develop strategies to overcome these obstacles and create a more supportive environment for your well-being. Embracing this reflective practice will not only help you prioritize self-care but also foster a greater sense of agency and resilience as you navigate the complexities of your life. Use this opportunity to explore the barriers that stand in your way and pave the path toward a more fulfilling and balanced existence.

In the journey of intentional motherhood, finding that balance is key. Embracing the idea that our well-being matters is not just a personal victory—it's a family triumph. It empowers us to create a nurturing environment where everyone's needs are acknowledged and met. As we fight the urge to always put our children first, let's remember that by taking care of ourselves, we are ultimately investing in our families' futures. Together, we can create a culture of health, happiness, and intentional living.

SHE IS WELL

What are the primary challenges you face in prioritizing your own well-being? Reflect on whether these challenges are self-imposed or genuinely unavoidable, and consider how this distinction might influence your ability to take care of yourself.

CHALLENGE

Self-imposed? ☐   Legitimate ☐

CHALLENGE

Self-imposed? ☐   Legitimate? ☐

CHALLENGE

Self-imposed? ☐   Legitimate? ☐

Family Engagement Opportunity

Family Well-Being

Draw a large circle on the poster board. Divide the circle into six segments, like slices of a pie. Label each segment with one of the following aspects of well-being- Physical Health, Emotional Health, Social Connections, Mental Health, Spiritual Health, and Financial Health. As a family, discuss each segment of the wheel. Then use consensus or a majority vote to capture your family's current level of well-being in each area on a scale of 1 to 10.

Chapter 11:
Fostering Growth Mindset in Your Children

"The best way to predict your future is to create it."

— Abraham Lincoln

Teaching Resilience and Adaptability

Teaching resilience and adaptability is a vital aspect of nurturing our children in an ever-changing world. As parents and professionals, we have the unique opportunity to guide the next generation through challenges, equipping them with the skills necessary to thrive amidst uncertainty. Resilience goes beyond simply bouncing back from adversity; it involves the ability to learn and grow from experiences, turning obstacles into means. By intentionally fostering these qualities in our children, we help them develop a robust foundation for navigating life's complexities.

One of the most powerful ways to teach resilience is through modeling our own responses to challenges. Children observe how we handle setbacks and stresses, often mirroring our behaviors and attitudes. When we approach difficulties with a growth mindset, demonstrating that failure is not the end but a valuable learning opportunity, we instill confidence in our children. Let them witness our determination and adaptability in the face of adversity and encourage them to share their own experiences. This open dialogue not only strengthens our bond but also empowers them to embrace challenges with a positive outlook.

Encouraging problem-solving skills is another essential component of teaching resilience. Instead of immediately providing solutions when our children encounter difficulties, we can guide them to think critically and explore various options. This process not only fosters independence but also cultivates creativity. By asking questions that prompt them to consider different perspectives, we help them build a toolkit of strategies for overcoming obstacles. Celebrate their efforts, regardless of the outcome, to reinforce the idea that resilience is about the journey, not just the destination.

Adaptability is closely linked to resilience, and it is crucial for our children to learn how to adjust their expectations and strategies in response to changing circumstances. Life is inherently unpredictable, and teaching our children to embrace flexibility will serve them well in all aspects of life.

Encourage them to step outside their comfort zones by trying new activities or facing new challenges. Celebrate their willingness to adapt, reinforcing the notion that growth often comes from pushing boundaries and stepping into the unknown. Help them see that change can lead to exciting opportunities, fostering a sense of adventure rather than fear.

Finally, instilling a sense of purpose can significantly enhance resilience and adaptability. When children understand their values and goals, they are more likely to navigate difficulties with determination and focus. Engage in discussions about their passions and aspirations, helping them connect their experiences to a broader context. Create a supportive environment where they feel safe to express themselves and explore their interests. By nurturing their sense of purpose, we empower our children to approach challenges with optimism and a belief in their ability to overcome any obstacle, ultimately transforming challenges into opportunities for growth.

To put this into practice, I invite you to engage in the upcoming self-reflection activity, which encourages you to try something new with your family. As you complete this adventure, take the time to examine the outcomes and the value of the experience—what worked, what didn't, and how it impacted your relationships. This reflective process will help you appreciate the joys of curiosity and the importance of learning, both as an individual and as a family unit.

SOMETHING NEW

Self-Reflection:

Brainstorm small challenges that require you and children to adapt or try something new, such as changing plans, going to some place new, or trying new foods. Reflect on the process, reactions and the outcome of each experience.

Encouraging Curiosity and Learning

Encouraging curiosity and learning in our children is one of the most profound gifts we can offer them. As parents and professionals invested in their growth, we have the unique opportunity to cultivate an environment where exploration and inquiry thrive. When we nurture curiosity, we ignite a love for learning that lasts a lifetime. This journey begins with recognizing the innate curiosity that exists within every child. By embracing their questions and encouraging them to seek answers, we foster an atmosphere of discovery that empowers them to explore the world around them.

To instill a sense of wonder, we must first model curiosity ourselves. Children are keen observers and often mirror our behaviors and attitudes. When we demonstrate an eagerness to learn—whether it's through reading, experimenting, or engaging in new experiences—we set a powerful example. Sharing our own questions and pursuits not only shows that learning is a lifelong endeavor but also invites our children to join us in this enriching journey. By discussing what excites us, we create a dynamic dialogue that encourages them to express their interests and inquiries freely.

Creating opportunities for hands-on experiences can further stimulate curiosity. Rather than presenting information in a traditional, static manner, we can engage our children through interactive activities that promote exploration. Nature walks, science experiments, or even cooking together can transform mundane tasks into exciting learning adventures. These experiences not only satisfy their curiosity but also deepen their understanding of concepts through practical application. By fostering an environment where questions lead to exploration, we empower our children to take charge of their learning journey.

To foster a more supportive and encouraging environment, consider these ideas:

- ❖ *Provide open-ended toys and materials:* Blocks, art supplies, and natural objects can spark imagination and creativity.

- ❖ *Make learning fun:* Play games, read books, and do activities that make learning enjoyable.

- ❖ *Travel:* Explore new places and cultures, even if it's just a day trip to a nearby town.

- ❖ *Visit museums and libraries:* These places offer a wealth of information and opportunities for learning.

- ❖ *Read aloud:* Start reading to your child from a young age. Choose books that are age-appropriate and interesting to them.

- ❖ *Encourage imaginative play:* Dress-up, pretend play, and storytelling can help children develop their creativity.

- ❖ *Provide art supplies:* Let your child experiment with different art materials, such as paint, crayons, and clay.

- ❖ *Play games that require problem-solving:* Puzzles, board games, and building toys can help children develop these skills.

It is equally important to celebrate the process of discovery, rather than merely focusing on outcomes. Each question our children ask and every attempt they make is a stepping stone in their learning path. By acknowledging their efforts and encouraging them to embrace mistakes as opportunities for growth, we help them develop resilience and a positive attitude toward challenges. This mindset reinforces the idea that learning is not just about right answers but about the journey of discovery itself. When we celebrate their curiosity, we validate their experiences and inspire them to continue seeking knowledge.

Finally, we must create a safe space for our children to explore their interests without fear of judgment. This involves embracing their unique perspectives and encouraging them to pursue their passions, no matter how unconventional they may seem. By allowing them the freedom to explore, we help them cultivate their identity and develop critical thinking skills. As parents and professionals, our role is to guide and support them while providing the tools they need to navigate their learning journey. Together, we can transform challenges into opportunities for growth, fostering a generation of lifelong learners eager to explore the boundless wonders of the world.

Family Engagement Opportunity

Wonder Wall

Designate a prominent spot in your home as the "Wonder Wall." This could be a section of a wall, a bulletin board, or a large piece of paper taped to a door. As a family, brainstorm a list of questions you have about the world around you. Encourage out-of-the-box thinking and questions that spark curiosity. Write each question on a sticky note and place it on the "Wonder Wall." Regularly revisit the "Wonder Wall" as a family. Choose a question to explore together. This could involve research, experiments, observations, or discussions.

Chapter 12:
Celebrating Small Victories

"Don't wait for the big things to happen before you celebrate.
Celebrate the small things; they are the big things."
— Robert Brault

Acknowledging Progress

Acknowledging progress is a vital aspect of the intentional motherhood journey, one that often gets overshadowed by the challenges we face. As parents and professionals, we frequently find ourselves entrenched in daily struggles, focusing on what still needs to be done rather than celebrating how far we have come. Embracing an attitude of gratitude for our progress not only uplifts our spirits but also empowers us to continue moving forward. Each small victory, whether it's a child mastering a new skill or a parent finding a moment of calm amidst chaos, deserves recognition. These milestones are not merely steps along our journey; they are affirmations of our resilience and growth.

In the hustle and bustle of our lives, it's easy to overlook the strides we make each day. However, taking a moment to reflect on our achievements can shift our perspective dramatically. Consider keeping a progress journal where you document both the big and small wins. Celebrate when your child shares their feelings openly or when you manage to carve out time for self-care despite an overwhelming schedule. This practice not only reinforces a positive mindset but also serves as a tangible reminder of the growth that occurs even in the toughest times. Acknowledging these moments fosters a sense of accomplishment that propels us forward.

As we shift our focus to celebrating progress, it's crucial to recognize the importance of acknowledging our achievements, no matter how small they may seem. Each task completed, each goal reached, and each moment of growth contributes to our overall journey as mothers and individuals. To facilitate this practice, I invite you to engage in the upcoming progress tracker activity. Over a designated period, you will capture your task achievements and accomplishments, reflecting on how each one has contributed to your personal and familial well-being. Additionally, take a moment to note whether you celebrated each achievement, reinforcing the value of recognizing your hard work. This exercise will not only help you stay motivated but will also cultivate a mindset of gratitude and self-appreciation, reminding you that progress is a vital part of both motherhood and personal growth.

ACHIEVEMENT TRACKER

PROGRESS/ACCOMPLISHMENT COMPLETE? CELEBRATED?

Moreover, recognizing progress is essential for cultivating a growth mindset in our children. When we model appreciation for our own journey, we teach our children the importance of resilience and perseverance. They learn that setbacks are not failures but opportunities to learn and grow. This shift in mindset can transform the way children approach challenges, encouraging them to embrace difficulties as part of their development. By celebrating progress together, we build a supportive environment where both parents and children feel valued and motivated to strive for their goals.

It is also crucial to connect with others on this journey. Sharing our experiences with fellow parents or professionals can amplify our sense of progress. Engaging in community discussions, whether through online forums or local support groups, allows us to gain different perspectives on our challenges and triumphs. Hearing how others navigate similar situations can provide inspiration and reassurance that we are not alone. Together, we can celebrate each other's victories, creating a collective atmosphere of encouragement and support that fuels our growth.

Ultimately, acknowledging progress is not just about celebrating success; it's about nurturing a spirit of gratitude and optimism in our lives. As we navigate the complexities of motherhood and professional responsibilities, let us commit to recognizing the small victories that illuminate our paths. In doing so, we cultivate resilience, foster growth in ourselves and our children, and inspire a community that thrives on positivity and encouragement. By intentionally celebrating our progress, we create a powerful momentum that fuels our journey toward becoming the best versions of ourselves.

Creating Family Rituals of Celebration

Creating family rituals of celebration is a powerful way to strengthen bonds, cultivate joy, and instill lasting values in our children. These rituals provide a framework for connection, allowing families to come together in meaningful ways. When we intentionally craft moments of celebration, we create a safe space where love and gratitude can flourish. Whether it's a weekly family dinner, a monthly game night, or an annual tradition that marks a significant event, these rituals become the fabric of family life, weaving together memories that last a lifetime.

Celebration rituals can be as simple or elaborate as families desire. The key is to embed intention into these practices. Consider what values are most important to your family— gratitude, resilience, creativity—and find ways to express these through celebration. For instance, a gratitude jar can be a beautiful ritual where family members write down things they are thankful for throughout the month, culminating in a special gathering to share and reflect. This not only reinforces the practice of gratitude but also fosters open communication and connection among family members, enriching their relationships.

Moreover, involving children in the creation of these rituals empowers them and enhances their sense of belonging within the family unit. When children contribute to the planning and execution of celebrations, they feel valued and heard. This could mean allowing them to choose the theme for a birthday party or deciding on the menu for a special family dinner. By engaging in this collaborative process, children learn important life skills, such as organization and teamwork, while also developing a deep appreciation for the traditions that shape their family identity.

As families navigate the complexities of life, these rituals serve as anchors, providing stabil and comfort in times of change. I must confess that navigating the transition of fam celebrations and rituals during my divorce process has been a deeply person and transformative experience. I vividly remember my first holidays alone, feeling t weight of solitude as I prepared a full spread of traditional dishes, a routine I h embraced while hosting our families and creating cherished memories with my childre

In those moments, I clung to the familiar comforts of my past, hoping to replicate the joy of family gatherings despite the absence of my loved ones. However, as one holiday alone turned into many, I began to realize that holding on to old traditions was not serving me well. Rather than unconsciously allowing the holidays be a reminder of what was lost, I decided to reenvision my approach.

I started to use these occasions as opportunities to engage more heavily with my community and extend my support to those around me. By sharing in new experiences, volunteering, and building relationships with neighbors, I discovered new ways to celebrate that not only honored my past but also fostered new connections that were meaningful in my present. This shift allowed me to redefine joy and gratitude, transforming what could have been a time of isolation into a chance to create new rituals that reflected my evolving life and the beautiful community I was becoming a part of.

No matter your circumstances, you may use the next activity to rethink your own celebrations and rituals. This exploration is particularly valuable during times of transition or disruption, as creating meaningful family rituals can provide a sense of stability and connection amidst change. Whether you're facing a major life event or simply navigating the everyday ups and downs, intentional rituals can offer comfort, strengthen bonds, and help your family build resilience together.

Essentially, celebrations can act as powerful reminders of the love that binds a family together, especially during challenging moments. In this way, rituals of celebration not only mark joyful occasions but also provide resilience—a reminder that families can face challenges united by love and shared experiences. Creating family rituals of celebration is an ongoing journey of growth and connection. These moments of joy help to cultivate a legacy of intentional living, teaching our children the importance of recognizing and honoring the milestones in their lives. As parents and professionals in the realms of life coaching and self-development, we have the unique opportunity to model this intentionality, transforming everyday moments into extraordinary celebrations no matter the circumstance. Embrace the potential of these rituals and watch as they cultivate a life filled with meaning, connection, and joy for you and your family.

RETHINKING TRADITIONS

Self-Reflection:

Consider your family traditions for a specific holiday or occasion. Reflect on changes that could make it more meaningful or intentional. In the case where a disruptive change has taken place that affects that occassion (e.g. death, child sharing, new family member, relocation, etc.), think specifically about adapting/coping to such change. Refer to your motherhood manifesto as needed.

Family Engagement Opportunity

<u>Winning Together</u>

Designate a space in your home, such as a bulletin board, to continually showcase and celebrate family achievements, no matter how big or small. This ongoing display fosters a sense of pride and encourages a culture of support within your family.

<u>Family Adventures</u>

Lead your family in the process of planning and implementing a new family ritual, such as a monthly movie night or a weekly game night. Collaboratively decide on the details, including themes, activities, and snacks, to ensure everyone feels included and invested in this new tradition.

Chapter 13:
Reflecting on Your Journey

"The unexamined life is not worth living."

—Socrates

The Importance of Reflection

Reflection is a powerful tool that allows us to pause amidst the chaos of daily life and gain clarity on our experiences. For parents and professionals alike, taking the time to reflect can illuminate the lessons hidden within our challenges. In the journey of motherhood, we often find ourselves caught up in routines, expectations, and responsibilities that can overshadow our personal growth. By embracing reflection, we create space for understanding, enabling us to transform obstacles into tools for greater self-awareness and fulfillment.

When we reflect, we engage in a meaningful dialogue with ourselves. This process encourages us to examine our thoughts, emotions, and actions with honesty and compassion. It is through this introspection that we can identify patterns in our behavior and recognize the areas in which we can grow. This might mean acknowledging the moments of frustration or self-doubt, while also celebrating the triumphs, no matter how small. Each reflection becomes a building block for resilience and a deeper connection to our values, guiding us in our parenting journey.

Reflection also fosters gratitude. Amid the whirlwind of parenting and professional obligations, it is easy to overlook the beauty in the everyday moments. Taking time to reflect allows us to shift our focus from what is lacking to what is abundant in our lives. By consciously acknowledging our successes and the joy found in our relationships, we cultivate a mindset that enhances our overall well-being. This practice not only enriches our lives but also sets a powerful example for our children, teaching them the importance of gratitude and mindfulness.

Moreover, the act of reflection can strengthen our decision-making skills. In parenting, we are often faced with choices that can significantly impact our families. By reflecting on past experiences, we can analyze what worked, what didn't, and why. This evaluation empowers us to make informed decisions that align with our goals and values. As professionals, this skill extends beyond our personal lives, enhancing our ability to lead with intention and empathy, creating a ripple effect that influences those around us.

As we begin approaching the conclusion of this journey together, it's essential to take a moment to revisit the self-reflections you've completed throughout this book. The next activity invites you to think about your insights, observations, and takeaways, allowing you to synthesize your growth and recognize the patterns that have emerged along the way. Taking the time to reflect on your experiences is not just a one-time exercise; it's a practice that can serve you well beyond the pages of this book. By regularly engaging in self-reflection, you cultivate a deeper understanding of your journey, celebrate your progress, and identify areas for continued growth. This intentional pause will empower you to carry forward the lessons learned, ensuring that you remain connected to your evolving self and your aspirations as a mother. So, grab whatever you feel you need, find a quiet space, and immerse yourself in this reflective process, acknowledging how far you've come and the beautiful path that lies ahead.

And remember, reflection is not just a passive activity; it is an intentional practice that fuels growth and transformation. For parents navigating the complexities of motherhood and professionals striving for balance, reflection offers a sanctuary of insight and clarity. It invites us to embrace our journeys with an open heart, recognizing that each challenge is an opportunity for learning. By prioritizing reflection, we can foster resilience, gratitude, and purposeful decision-making, ultimately enriching our lives and the lives of those we love.

REFLECTION RETREAT

Self-Reflection:

Take the time to revisit your past reflections for a moment of introspection and self-care. Consider whether you notice any recurring patterns or themes in your thoughts and experiences. Are there specific insights or lessons that stand out?

Journaling for Growth

Journaling for growth is a powerful practice that can transform your experience as a parent and a professional. It offers a space for reflection, allowing you to process your daily challenges and triumphs in a meaningful way. As you put pen to paper, you create a dialogue with yourself that can illuminate your thoughts, feelings, and aspirations. This process not only helps you gain clarity about your personal journey but also enhances your ability to nurture and guide your children through theirs. By committing to regular journaling, you invite growth into your life, turning obstacles into a means for becoming the intentional mother you aspire to be.

In the hustle and bustle of daily life, it is easy to overlook the significance of your own thoughts and emotions. Journaling provides a sanctuary where you can explore these inner landscapes without judgment. When you dedicate time to write, you enable yourself to step back from the chaos, allowing for deeper understanding and insights. This practice can uncover patterns in your behavior and reactions, helping you to identify areas where you can grow. The act of writing becomes a form of self-coaching, empowering you to take charge of your narrative and embrace the evolution that comes with motherhood.

Moreover, journaling serves as a historical record of your experiences and growth. As you document milestones, setbacks, and revelations, you create a treasure trove of wisdom that you and your children can revisit in the future. Reflecting on past entries can reveal how much you have learned and how far you have come, fostering a sense of resilience. This archive not only reinforces your personal development but also models the importance of self-reflection to your children, teaching them the value of their own stories and the lessons that come from them.

Journaling can take many forms, allowing you to find a style that resonates with your personality and preferences. Each approach offers unique benefits, enabling you to explore your thoughts and emotions in a way that feels authentic to you.

Here are some creative journaling styles to consider:

- ❖ *Stream of Consciousness:* Writing continuously for a set period without worrying about grammar or structure, allowing your thoughts to flow freely.

- ❖ *Gratitude Journaling:* Regularly jotting down things you are grateful for, fostering a positive mindset and appreciation for life's small joys.

- ❖ *Bullet Journaling:* Using bullet points and symbols to create an organized system for tracking tasks, goals, and reflections, combining planning with personal insights.

- ❖ *Art Journaling:* Incorporating drawings, sketches, or collages alongside your written entries to express emotions and thoughts visually.

- ❖ *Prompt Journaling:* Using specific prompts or questions to guide your writing, helping you dive deeper into your feelings and experiences.

- ❖ *Dream Journaling:* Recording your dreams upon waking, exploring their meanings and insights into your subconscious mind.

- ❖ *Mind Mapping:* Creating visual diagrams that connect ideas and concepts, facilitating a more dynamic exploration of your thoughts.

Experimenting with different journaling styles can enhance your self-reflection practice, making it a more engaging and enriching experience. Whether you prefer the simplicity of bullet points or the creativity of art journaling, the key is to find a method that resonates with you and encourages a deeper connection to your thoughts and feelings. Essentially, journaling for growth is about embracing the journey. It's a commitment to understanding yourself better, nurturing your emotional health, and fostering deeper connections with your children.

As you write, you become an active participant in your own transformation, turning challenges into opportunities for growth. This practice is not merely a means of coping with the demands of motherhood and professional life; it is a profound tool for intentional living. By prioritizing journaling, you not only enrich your own life but also pave the way for your children to grow into reflective, resilient individuals.

In our next activity, we will take a refreshing departure from the traditional journaling styles explored throughout this book by engaging in a creative journaling exercise. This activity invites you to express your thoughts and feelings in a more artistic and imaginative way, allowing for a unique exploration of your inner world. You can choose any creative approach that resonates with you—whether it's drawing, painting, collage-making, or even crafting a poem or story. The goal is to respond to the provided prompt through your chosen medium, thereby unlocking new perspectives and insights that may not emerge through standard writing. The included page can be used for this exercise or serve as a placeholder for brainstorming and planning. In any case, embrace this opportunity to let your creativity flow and discover the healing power of artistic expression as you reflect on your journey.

CREATIVE CAPTURE

Explore alternative journaling styles by experimenting with creative forms such as drawing, painting, poetry, or collage. Use one of these mediums to respond to the following prompt:

**"What are my hopes and dreams for my children
and how can I support their development?"**

Family Engagement Opportunity

Family Reflection Circle

Choose a comfortable and quiet space in your home where everyone can gather. Prepare a list of reflection prompts that each family member can respond to. Take turns sharing responses to the prompts. Conclude the activity by inviting each family member to express one takeaway from the discussion and one positive affirmation for themselves or someone else in the group.

Chapter 14:
Moving Forward with Intention

"By failing to prepare, you are preparing to fail."
— Benjamin Franklin

Creating an Action Plan

Creating an action plan is a pivotal step in transforming the challenges of motherhood into opportunities for growth. It begins with a clear vision of what you want to achieve as a parent, professional, and individual. This vision acts as a guiding star, illuminating the path forward amidst the chaos of daily life. This is a good time to revisit the Motherhood Manifesto you created at the beginning of this book.

Developing a strong vision for your motherhood action plan begins with a deep understanding of your values, aspirations, and the unique dynamic of your family. Using everything we've covered, begin by envisioning the kind of mother you aspire to be and the environment you wish to create for your children—consider what qualities you want to embody and the experiences you want to share with them. Reflect on your long-term goals, both for yourself and your family, and think about how these goals align with your core values, such as connection, compassion, and growth. To bring this vision to life, outline specific, actionable steps that will guide you in achieving these goals, whether that means prioritizing quality time, fostering open communication, or encouraging exploration and learning. Visualize the milestones you want to celebrate along the way, and remember to remain flexible, allowing your vision to evolve as your children grow and your circumstances change. This vision will serve as a compass, guiding your decisions and actions while nurturing a fulfilling and intentional motherhood journey.

Once you have defined your vision, break it down into manageable, achievable goals. Consider the various dimensions of your life: your relationships, personal growth, career aspirations, and your role as a mother. Use the next activity to ensure that these goals are specific, measurable, attainable, relevant, and time-bound—commonly known as SMART goals. When you clarify what success looks like in each area, you create a roadmap that helps you stay focused and motivated. This structure not only empowers you but also serves as a model for your children, teaching them the value of setting and pursuing goals.

A SMART GOAL

Create one SMART goal (Specific, Measurable, Attainable, Relevant, Time-bound) for embracing the next chapter of your motherhood journey.

 **SPECIFIC**

What do I want to happen?

 **MEASUREABLE**

How will I know when I have achieved my goal?

 **ATTAINABLE**

Is the goal realistic and how will I accomplish it?

 **RELEVANT**

Why is my goal important to me?

 **TIME-BOUND**

What is my deadline for this goal?

Next, outline the specific actions you need to take to reach these goals. This can include daily routines, new habits, or skills you wish to develop. Perhaps you want to incorporate mindfulness practices into your parenting, or maybe you aim to enhance your professional skills while balancing family life. Identify the resources you need, whether they are books, workshops, or support networks. By creating a list of actionable steps, you transform abstract goals into concrete tasks that can be tackled one at a time. Each small success builds your confidence and momentum, reinforcing your commitment to intentional living.

Accountability plays a crucial role in executing your action plan. Share your goals with a trusted friend, partner, or mentor who can offer support and encouragement. Regular check- ins can help you stay on track, celebrate your achievements, and reassess your strategies if necessary. Additionally, consider joining a community of like-minded individuals who are also on a journey of self-discovery and growth. The power of shared experiences can provide inspiration, motivation, and the reassurance that you are not alone in your challenges.

Finally, remain flexible and open to adjustments along the way. Life as a parent is often unpredictable, and your initial action plan may need to evolve as circumstances change. Embrace the idea that growth is a journey, not a destination. Reflect on your progress regularly and be willing to adapt your strategies as needed. This resilience not only enhances your effectiveness as a mother and professional but also models an essential life skill for your children. By creating a dynamic action plan, you foster an environment of growth and intention that empowers both you and your family to thrive amidst challenges.

Embracing the Next Chapter of Motherhood

Embracing the next chapter of motherhood can often feel like standing at the edge of a vast, uncharted territory. The anticipation of new experiences is often dampened by the weight of numerous barriers. Some of these barriers are tangible and real: the demands of work, the needs of other children, or even the unpredictability of daily life. Yet, many of the obstacles we face are self-imposed, born from our own fears and internal narratives. As we navigate this journey, it becomes crucial to recognize both the external challenges and the internal dialogues that keep us from progressing.

In this transformative phase, the concept of availability emerges as a significant factor. Life as a parent is often a jigsaw puzzle of responsibilities where time feels scarce. Small windows of opportunity appear fleetingly, and it's essential to seize them with intention. These moments may be brief, perhaps a quiet morning before the day begins or a few minutes while dinner simmers on the stove. By recognizing and valuing these small intervals, we can create the space needed for personal growth and exploration. Embracing these moments is not just about filling time; it's about enriching our lives and acknowledging that even the smallest steps can lead to significant changes.

Working new tasks and functions into an already busy life can feel overwhelming. The key lies in integrating these new elements with existing responsibilities rather than viewing them as separate burdens. For instance, use the next activity to consider how to weave in self-care practices or personal development activities into daily routines. This might mean listening to an inspiring podcast during your commute or practicing mindfulness while doing household chores. By reshaping our perspective on how we allocate time and energy, we can foster an environment where growth becomes a natural part of our daily lives rather than a daunting afterthought.

In the next activity, you will focus on identifying "low-hanging fruit" to optimize your time. Consider how you can start leveraging these kinds of opportunities in your daily routines.

S M T W T F S

DATE :

AVAILABILITY AUDIT

TO-DO LIST

Take one day and track your "idle" time. Are there pockets of time throughout the day that can be used for personal growth, self-care or pursuing your interests?

OPPORTUNITIES

NOTES

As we strive to embrace change, it's also vital to cultivate a mindset that welcomes imperfection. The journey of motherhood is not about achieving a flawless balance but rather about being flexible and adaptable. Accepting that there will be setbacks and days when things don't go as planned allows us to approach challenges with resilience. Each stumble is an opportunity to learn and grow, reinforcing the idea that motherhood is a dynamic process. By embracing our imperfections, we can find strength in vulnerability and inspire those around us to do the same.

Remarkably, embracing the next chapter of motherhood is a profound journey of self- discovery and empowerment. As we face both real and self-actualized barriers, we have the opportunity to redefine our narratives and create a life that aligns with our values and aspirations. The path may be fraught with challenges, but every step taken intentionally brings us closer to a more fulfilled version of ourselves. By embracing change with courage and compassion, we not only transform our own lives but also set an inspiring example for our children, teaching them the importance of resilience, adaptability, and the joy of personal growth.

As you conclude this book, take a moment to reflect on the insights and value you have gained from your exploration of intentional motherhood. What key lessons resonated with you, and how have they shifted your perspective on your role as a mother? Consider how these newfound understandings will influence the next chapter of your motherhood journey. What specific actions or changes do you plan to implement in your parenting approach, and how will you nurture the relationships and systems around you? Write down your thoughts and commit to embracing this renewed perspective as you move forward.

MOVING FORWARD

Self-Reflection:
What key lessons resonated with you, and how have they shifted your perspective on your role as a mother? What specific actions or changes do you plan to implement in your parenting approach, and how will you nurture the relationships and systems around you?

Family Engagement Opportunity

Mission Possible

As a family, brainstorm a list of goals you would like to achieve together. For each goal, brainstorm specific actions you can take as a family to achieve it. Discuss when you will start working on each goal and how often you will work on it. As you achieve each goal, celebrate your success as a family.

www.ingramcontent.com/pod-product-compliance
Lightning Source LLC
Chambersburg PA
CBHW061757120626
46550CB00005B/2033